Adam Harkness

Iroquois High School, 1845-1895

A Story of Fifty Years

Adam Harkness

Iroquois High School, 1845-1895
A Story of Fifty Years

ISBN/EAN: 9783744764117

Printed in Europe, USA, Canada, Australia, Japan

Cover: Foto ©ninafisch / pixelio.de

More available books at **www.hansebooks.com**

SCHOOL

1845–1895

A STORY OF FIFTY YEARS

BY

ADAM HARKNESS.

TORONTO:
WILLIAM BRIGGS
WESLEY BUILDINGS.

PREFACE.

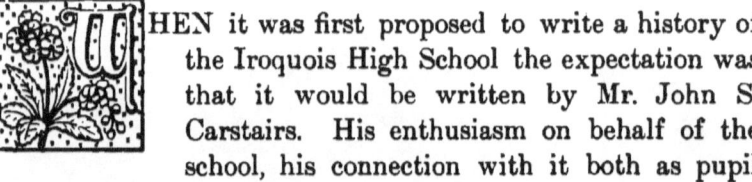HEN it was first proposed to write a history of the Iroquois High School the expectation was that it would be written by Mr. John S. Carstairs. His enthusiasm on behalf of the school, his connection with it both as pupil and teacher, and his experience in and capacity for literary work, all marked him out as the one best equipped for the task. But, after he became Principal of the Stirling High School, at the commencement of the Fall term in 1894, it became obvious to the promoters of the undertaking, that they must look elsewhere for a historian.

The committee having the matter in charge, and of which I was the chairman, then made an effort to get old students to contribute reminiscences that could be easily arranged, so that, with the illustrations, an interesting volume might be produced. However, the notices sent out with this object in view met a very inadequate response, and there seemed to be no one specially fitted for the work who could give it the required attention. In the meantime the contributions to cover the cost of publication were coming in apace, making it necessary to get the book prepared. As there did not appear to be any other person available, I was induced, by my colleagues on the committee and some other friends of the enterprise, to do the writing, as my contribution to the Jubilee Fund of the High School.

It has been in a great measure a labor of love. Though

never connected with the school in any other way than as a citizen, I had from the outside watched its course during most of the fifty years of its history. I had known Mr. Dick when, as local superintendent, he visited our little country school in 1850. Except Mr. Davies, with whom my acquaintance was slight, I had numbered among my personal friends every succeeding headmaster. One brother and sister were among Mr. Dick's pupils, another brother with Mr. Albert Carman, and still another and three of my own children with Mr. Whitney. In addition, a large proportion of my contemporaries, and the friends who helped to brighten the days as they went by, had at one time or another been pupils of the school.

For much of the period covered I found my data rather scanty. Mrs. William L. Redmond kindly gave me access to the papers of her father, Mr. Philip Carman. These covered the first ten years, but from that down to very recent times I was confined almost entirely to the minutes and accounts of the School Board, returns to the Government, and my own knowledge of local history.

The speeches and papers of the three headmasters, one assistant, and the chairman of the Board, given in the Appendix, it is hoped will make good some of the shortcomings in the body of the work, resulting from my want of familiarity with the inside life of the school.

ADAM HARKNESS.

IROQUOIS, *January 28th,* 1896.

CONTENTS.

CHAPTER I.

Early History—The Camp Meeting—The Little Log School-House—The Schoolmasters—The Old School-House - - 9–14

CHAPTER II.

Farming Storekeepers—Beginning of the Village—John J. Kerr—First Efforts to Establish a High School - - - - 15–18

CHAPTER III.

First Building—Early Settlers—The Founders of the School—John A. Carman—Matthew and James Coons—First Trustees—George Brouse—Jacob Brouse—John P. Crysler—J. W. Rose—Rev. Wm. Shorts—Philip Carman - - - 19–25

CHAPTER IV.

First School—Engaging the Principal—The Curriculum—Fees—Mr. Gates—Miss Bailey—Mr. Truax—School Diaries—Visitors—First Pupils - - - - - - - - 26–31

CHAPTER V.

Mr. Dick—Examinations—How Teachers were Appointed—Condition of the County—Prizes—County and Local Boards of Trustees—New School Law—Wm. Elliot—Robert Lowery—Ryerson's Visit—Public Library Established - - - 32–39

CHAPTER VI.

Albert Carman—General Prosperity—James Croil—J. S. Ross—Effect of their Appointment—Protracted Meeting—Disciplining a Student—The Methodist Church—Belleville Seminary—Retirement of Mr. Carman - - - - - 40-45

CHAPTER VII.

Davies and Cowan—Changes in the School—Mr. Laing—Incorporation of the Village—Retirement of Mr. Davies—Mr. Cowan engaged—New Trustees—A. B. Sherman—Alex. McDonell—Dr. Worthington—Dr. Williams—Local Aid—*Laissez faire*—The Revenues—County Grants - - - 46-55

CHAPTER VIII.

Mr. Whitney—Farming Out the School—Miss Bailey—Success—Government Grants—Local Apathy—The Morrisburg School—Changes in the Law—Formation of High School Districts—Model School—Abolition of the Districts - - 56-64

CHAPTER IX.

Mr. Whitney (*continued*)—Revenues and Salaries—Assistants—New Trustees—Edward Parlow—Robert Toye—Solomon Doran—James Stephenson, M.D.—John N. Tuttle—John Harkness, M.D.—Geo. Steacy, M.D.—James A. Carman, B.A.—Declining Prosperity—The New Woman—Public Buildings—School Neglected - - - - - - 65-75

CHAPTER X.

Mr. Whitney (*continued*)—Want of Equipment—New Assistants—Wm. Montgomery—Chas. Potter—Inspectors' Reports—Business Outlook Improving—Added Trustees—Cephas and Mason Mills—Beginning of Trouble—Close of Whitney regime - - - - - - - - - - 76-85

CHAPTER XI.

James A. Carman—A New Era—A. C. Casselman—Erection of the New Building—Its Effect on the School—Becomes a Three-Master School—Ralph Ross—The Three C's—J. S. Carstairs—Inspectors' Reports—Increased Attendance—Sources of Revenue - - - - - - - - - 86-93

CONTENTS.   vii

CHAPTER XII.

PAGE

James A. Carman (*continued*)—Changes—Retirement of Casselman—Four Masters—Criticisms—Newspaper Enterprise—Trouble in the School—Mr. Thompson—Mr. Knox—Mr. Coulter—Election Contest—Retirement of Carman and Carstairs—Death of John A. Carman - - - 94–102

CHAPTER XIII.

Joseph A. Jackson—New Regime—Mr. Knox—Miss Hare—Miss Ross—Mr. Warren—Miss Dillabough—Continued Progress—Present Board—Dr. Harkness—R. M. Bouck—Howard Durant—J. N. Forward—N. G. Sherman—Edward McNulty—Headmasters and Assistants—Revenues and Salaries—General Results—New Features - 103–115

CHAPTER XIV.

Alumni - - - - - - - - - - - 116–126

CHAPTER XV.

The Reunion - - - - - - - - - - 127–132

APPENDIX.

Introductory—Dr. Carman—W. A. Whitney—James A. Carman—J. S. Carstairs—Dr. Harkness - - - - 133–161

Semi-Centennial of Iroquois High School.

CHAPTER I.

Early History—The Camp Meeting—The Little Log School-House—The Schoolmasters—The Old School-House.

HE basin of the great lakes of North America has, and not inaptly, been described as an immense saucer, the rim of which rises in several places but slightly above the water.
Where this water found an outlet during the earlier period of the world's history has not been definitely determined, but it is pretty certain that, speaking geologically, it was not until comparatively recent years, or subsequent to the Glacial period, that it overflowed at Niagara, and passed down or cut out the St. Lawrence River. The first considerable barrier it met after passing Lake Ontario and its eastern extension, the Lake of the Thousand Islands, was what is now known as the Galops-Rapids.

A few miles east of this, and directly in the path of the stream, lay a huge moraine, about one hundred feet in height, and nearly a mile in diameter, left by the receding ice. The incoming flood found its way on either side of this, thus forming an island; but underlying the northern channel was a bed of limestone rock, which resisted the attrition of the water, while the bed of the southern channel, being of softer material, gradually deepened until the island became a point surrounded on the north side by a swamp.

Tradition says this isolated point was a favorite resort of the Indians; that amidst its groves of pine and maple they built their camp fires and held their Councils, and that the early French *voyageurs*, as they passed up and down between Montreal and the lakes, noted the conspicuous feature in the landscape, and named it after the most warlike tribe or confederation of red men that hunted along the St. Lawrence, calling it " Point Iroquois."

When, near the close of the eighteenth century, the country bordering on the north side of the St. Lawrence was settled, the river road was built through the swamp at the eastern and western extremities, and carried over the northern end of this point. The vicinity of the road, perhaps because of its greater elevation and natural beauty, probably also because it was a convenient place for those living to the east and west to meet, was early selected as the site of a church and burying-ground.

In 1823, under the supervision of William H. Williams, a youthful and zealous Methodist missionary, the first camp meeting, in the eastern part of what was then Upper Canada, was held in the grove or woods to the south of this road. The country folk for miles around gathered in from day to day, and from night to night—some to scoff, and some to pray; some, no doubt, from idle curiosity or a desire to break the monotony of their lives and mingle with their fellows. Many of them remained for weeks, returning home at intervals, or leaving some one in charge of their premises. Whatever may have been their object in coming, they generally learned to pray before they returned. The meeting left an impress on the character of the people that is yet plainly visible, and that has been far-reaching in its effects. Nearly all the old men living at the middle of the century dated their conversion from that " season of prayer," and the vicinity has continued to be a sort of centre from which Methodism has radiated.

More than half a century after Mr. Williams had so stirred the hearts of the people, his son, Dr. T. G. Williams, now of Sherbrooke, Que., but then of Iroquois, initiated and guided a movement that led to the union of the several branches of the Methodist Church in Canada.

The St. Lawrence River was, of course, the principal means of communication and channel of trade with the outside world; but the Galops was only one of a succession of rapids between Montreal and Lake Ontario, that made navigation very difficult; and early in the thirties a canal, or rather series of canals, designed to overcome these obstructions, was commenced.

The Iroquois or Galops Canal passed down the swamp or old channel of the river to the north of the "point," and terminated at its eastern extremity, where the locks were placed, and where the water-power thus created was utilized to drive two or three mills, around which the village of Iroquois was built. Previous to the building of the canal the front road was dotted with stores, but almost immediately thereafter the business centred round the mills. The village became the principal, almost the only trading, as well as milling and shipping, point, for a considerable section of country.

The country along the river and for two or three concessions back, was first settled by U.E. Loyalist soldiers and their families, that came over at the close of the Revolutionary war in 1784. The rear part of the front Township, and the Township in the rear of it, were subsequently occupied, partly by descendants of the first settlers, who had been less fortunate or less successful than their neighbors, and had been compelled to move inland, where land was cheaper, and partly by immigrants, these latter principally from the North of Ireland. Most of the settlers came from what might be termed educating countries. Whether from New England or New York, from Ireland or Scotland, they had learned to value education, and one of their first cares was to provide the means of preventing their children from growing up altogether unlettered. This could not be done without considerable exertion on the part of the parents, and some personal sacrifice.

The school-houses were built either in the centre of some settlement, or at a "cross-roads," where three or four of the small settlements could be accommodated. They were almost invariably of logs, and were generally from eighteen to twenty-four feet square, and about seven or eight feet in height to the eaves. The writer has a very distinct recollection of one that may serve as a sample. It was placed in the centre of a large wood, more than half a mile from any house, and where two roads crossed, or four roads met, and it accommodated the clearings or settlements on each of these roads, the children being required to travel generally from a mile to a mile and a half. It was eighteen feet square, built of dressed logs, rather neatly dovetailed at the corners, and the interstices between the logs chinked and plastered. It was floored and ceiled, the ceiling being slightly over six feet from the floor. The roof, what is called a square one, was shingled. In the centre of each end and of the back was a long, low window, while the front was occupied by a similar window near one corner, and a door near the other—this latter window was for the "master," while the others were intended to light the desks, which extended all the way along the back and across the ends until they passed the windows. The larger pupils, that were writing and "cyphering," used these desks, sitting on boards, with their faces to the wall, while the smaller ones occupied low benches ranged around the stove, which occupied the centre of the room. The teacher had a chair and a little table in the corner by the front window, and the corner behind the door held the wood-pile, a broom, and sometimes a water-pail. The house had been built by the neighbors, the logs being cut in the surrounding bush. One would furnish a few boards, another a few shingles. Just how the nails were paid for we never learned, but one old gentleman, who had lost his wife and quit housekeeping, furnished the little table which was the only piece of painted furniture in the room. In this room gathered daily, during a considerable portion of the year, twenty to thirty pupils between the ages of five and fifteen, and during the winter and spring months a few that were nearly grown men and women.

The teachers, until near the middle of the century, were nearly all Old Country people,—mostly men who had received a fair education, but had missed, or made shipwreck of, their chances in life, came to this country, and not being adapted to farming, resorted to teaching as a means of livelihood. The parents paid whatever might be agreed upon per month for each child; there was a small grant from the Government, and the teacher, unless he had a family, "boarded round." The books were such as each parent provided for his children, and those bought for the eldest were handed down from child to child until the whole family was served. The system was primitive, but the results were not altogether unsatisfactory. Among the books used were the old English Reader, Mavor's Spelling Book, a variety of arithmetics—among which Walkingame's figured conspicuously, Murray's and Lennie's Grammar, sometimes a book on higher mathematics, perhaps furnished by the teacher, and in some schools "Testaments," as the New Testament was designated. The literature of the readers was mostly from the writers of the early part of the eighteenth century. The teachers, much as has been said in their disparagement, were frequently men of considerable cultivation. They had seen something of the world, and in many instances had mixed with men of culture. When they "boarded round" they were usually—the men especially—welcome guests in the homes where they stayed, and it is not unreasonable to suppose that their presence in a family raised and, so to speak, widened the tone of the conversation. In most families the conversation is confined to matters of interest to the several members about the house or place, or in the neighborhood. In many cases the mind of the father, though it may be fairly well stored, is a sealed book to the children; the presence of a stranger of a little better, or at least different, culture, tends to draw out any members of the family that have anything to impart; experiences are related, strange and distant scenes are described, and the interest of the younger members of the family aroused. In addition to this, the co-operation of several neighbors in the organization and management of a school has an educational influence in itself. At their school-meetings they could discuss their ways and means just as deliberative bodies do that have larger interests under their control. They provided for the school directly, and to a large extent managed and guided its course, and, though it might be vastly inferior in many respects to what is demanded by more modern standards, it was their own school, and their interest in it created a love for education and a desire among the people to promote the interest of the school, which have made the work of the modern organizer not only easy but rich in results.

CHAPTER II.

Farming Storekeepers—Beginning of the Village—John J. Kerr—First Efforts to Establish a High School.

HE best of these schools were along the front or river road. The concession along the river was the first taken up, and in the front of Matilda Township the land was nearly all good; moreover, the road along which the stage passed on its way between Montreal and Kingston was during the earlier years of the century almost the only road that was passable at all seasons. The business of the country was done principally by the most enterprising residents on this road. In most instances the farmer would build his "store" near his residence, and carry on both store and farm; and these farming storekeepers, many of whom became wealthy, assumed to some extent the character of an aristocracy. From these families the Justices of the Peace, the Militia officers, the Court and School Commissioners, and, of course, the Members of the Legislative Assembly (or Parliament) were selected.

Peter Shaver, who lived about two miles east of the site of the present village, represented the County from 1824 to 1840, and George Brouse also represented it from 1828 to 1830; from 1828 to the time of the Union of the two Canadas, Dundas sent two members, and Mr. Brouse was elected along with Mr. Shaver in 1828, but the death of George IV. soon after necessitated a new election, and a Williamsburg man, John Cook, took his place. But it was not until near the middle of the century that any European immigrant, any one not "of the Pale," or any "bushwhacker," as residents of the back concessions were designated, was elected or appointed to any office higher than that of Path-master, Pound-keeper or School Trustee. As has been said, these stores and business places were scattered along the road at intervals, but, even before the canal was built—perhaps not before it was projected—the east end of Point Iroquois swamp, or rather the land adjoining, began to give evidence of becoming the site of a village. In 1827, the Post-office, the only one in the two western townships of the county, which had been kept by Mr. Glassford, near the eastern side, was secured by Mr. George Brouse and brought here. Here the steamboat landing was situated, a mill, a couple of stores, and a tavern. And here, about or a little before 1840, was built the first stone school-house in the Township of Matilda.

About this time a Mr. John J. Kerr was employed to teach the school. He was an Irishman who had received a liberal education, and who soon placed his school on a plane far above that of the ordinary schools, and who, we have reason to believe, did much to create in the community a desire for higher education. This is evidenced by the following correspondence, which, through the kindness of Dr. J. George Hodgins, of the Education Department, we have been enabled to procure:

MATILDA, *January 5th*, 1843.

SIR,—We, the undersigned commissioners for the Township of Matilda, beg leave to address you, as Superintendent of Education for Canada West, that we may obtain certain information that we require in relation to establishing a Grammar School in this place, which information we are desirous to obtain as soon as practicable, so that no time may be lost in acting upon it, as the materials that may be necessary for any additional buildings can be procured best during the sleighing season.

We will first give you a brief account of the present School, being composed of School Division No. 3, first concession of Matilda, very pleasantly situated on the Bank of the River St. Lawrence, a few rods from the steamboat landing, in a densely settled neighborhood, the inhabitants taking a lively interest in the education of their youths; and they have manifested that interest in a very

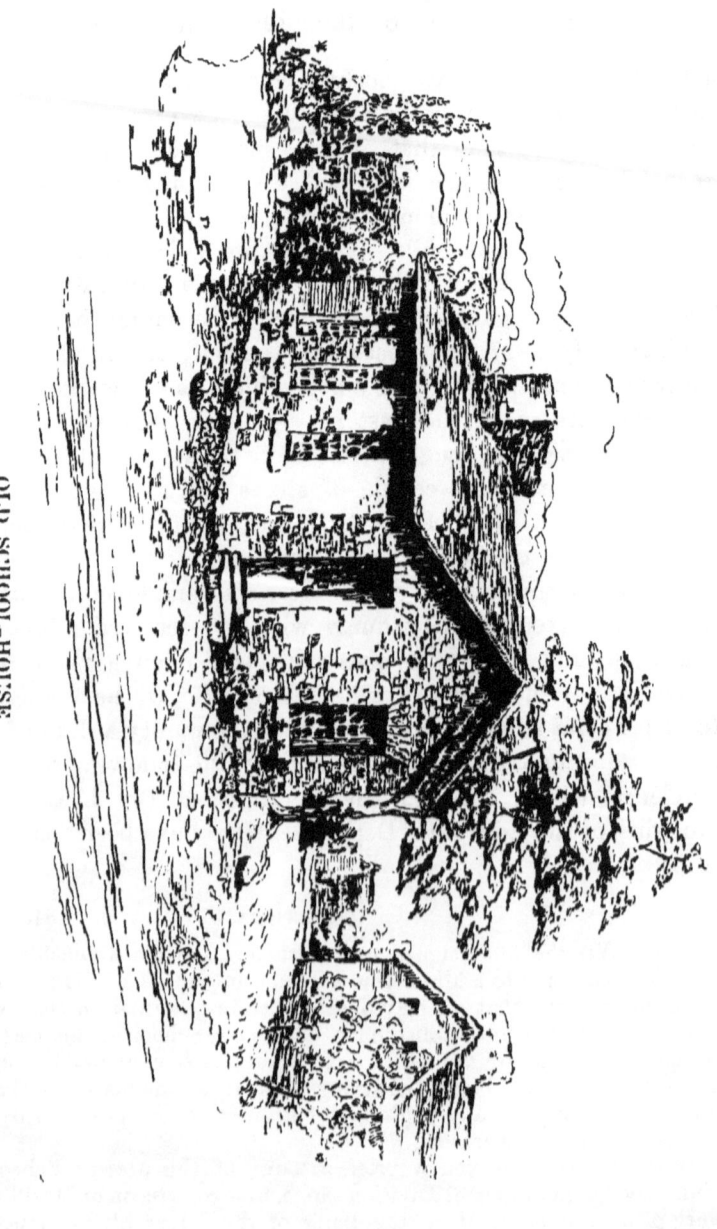

OLD SCHOOL-HOUSE.

handsome manner in the erection of the present building, being made of stone, 24 x 36 feet, divided into three rooms very comfortably finished, and they (the inhabitants) offer to add any other buildings that may be required to constitute it a Grammar School, agreeable to the sixth Section of the School Lands Act, providing said buildings do not cost over £200. The present School has been kept constantly for the last two years and upwards at the expense of £60 per annum for Teacher alone. The Teacher, John J. Kerr, Esquire, is a gentleman who has formerly been an Officer in the British Army, and who is amply qualified, to which the progress of his pupils gives ample testimony, having advanced even beyond the most sanguine expectations of their parents. The number in daily attendance has been from thirty to forty, and they have now advanced to upwards of fifty scholars, with still further applications for admittance, which would readily be admitted was the School properly established and the proper assistance afforded.

The following are the subjects upon which we beg to be instructed:

1. By whom will the house and appendages be held in trust, the School Commissioners of the Township or by a Board of Trustees appointed by the subscribers?

2. Who will have the management and control of the School?

3. Will the Grammar School exclude us from the benefits to be derived from the Common School Fund?

4. Will you be pleased to instruct us in the best and most suitable plan for the enlargement of the building?

5. What branches will be taught in the Grammar School?

6. Can we not become a Grammar School at once, and still proceed to erect additional buildings that may be necessary for permanently establishing said School?

7. Please to direct us upon any other points that may be necessary that you think will aid us in establishing a Grammar School.

We are the more anxious on this subject, being situated at the extremity of the District, being a distance of thirty-five miles from the District Town, thereby being deprived of the benefits of the District Town School.

We have the honor to submit the above queries to your consideration, having no other object in view than to advance Education amongst us, which is very much wanted.

We are,

Your obedient, humble servants,

PHILIP CARMAN.
GEORGE BROUSE.
CHARLES C. ROSE.

To the REVEREND J. MURRAY,
Superintendent of Education, Canada West.

[REPLY.]

EDUCATION OFFICE,
KINGSTON, *7th January*, 1843.

GENTLEMEN,—I have the honor to acknowledge the receipt of your letter of the 5th inst., containing queries respecting a Grammar School.

In reply I have to state that my powers are not by the present School Bill extended to Grammar Schools, and I cannot, therefore, give any very satisfactory information respecting them.

I may mention, however, that many applications have been made under the Bill 4th and 5th Victoria, Chapter 19, without having received any assistance for the support of Grammar Schools, but not being within my department, I do not know the reason why the moneys are not paid as provided for. You should apply to the Secretary West in the first place, and ascertain if the provisions of the Bill can yet be realized.

I have the honor to be, Sirs,
Your obedient servant,
(Signed) ROBERT MURRAY.

MESSRS. CARMAN, ROSE, ETC.,
School Commissioners, Matilda.

Messrs. Carman, Brouse and Rose appear to have been School Commissioners—probably appointed under the Act of 1841, which made more liberal provision for Government aid to education. The few Grammar Schools then in the country had been established under an Act passed in 1807, and were confined entirely to District, or what would now be called County towns. It is noticeable that the early efforts to promote education in this country were directed principally to the establishment of high grade schools. The first effort in behalf of common schools was made in 1816, when a grant equivalent to about $1.25 per year for each pupil attending was provided. Under this most of the common schools in this part of the country were established. The Act of 1841 not only made more liberal provision, but provided a more complete organization for the management of the schools. Its aim, however, appears to have been mainly to improve the Common School system, and the effort made to convert the Public school into a Grammar school proved for the time unsuccessful.

JAMES COONS, JOHN A. CARMAN, MATTHEW COONS.

CHAPTER III.

First Building—Early Settlers—The Founders of the School—John A. Carman—Matthew and James Coons—First Trustees—George Brouse—Jacob Brouse—John P. Crysler—J. W. Rose—Rev. Wm. Shorts—Philip Carman.

N common with the whole eastern part of Ontario bordering on the St. Lawrence, the Township of Matilda, in which the village of Iroquois is situated, and of which it formed a part until incorporated as a village in 1857, was first settled by disbanded soldiers who had adhered to the British side during the war of the Revolution. The four lots, comprising about 1,200 acres, now included within the limits of the village, were in 1786, two years after the settlement, owned by Dorothy and Michael Russell, Peter Murray, Martin Walter, Elizabeth and Peter Brouse, Jacob Coons and Michael Carman. The four first-named appear to have been crowded out, for pretty early in the century we find nearly the whole of this property divided pretty equally between the representatives of the other three families, who had, by intermarriage of the elder members, all become cousins either in the first or second degree. These families all belonged to the class described in a previous chapter—a class whose business training, whose contact with the outside world as merchants and lumbermen, naturally imbued them with a desire to provide a means for the better education of their children. No doubt many of them had felt the embarrassment resulting from their own educational shortcomings when called upon to fill positions of trust or honor, and it is not, therefore, surprising

that they should have endeavored to avail themselves of what appeared to be an opportunity to secure the means of procuring a better education, within their own neighborhood, than it was possible to procure in a common school. But what is surprising, is that, having failed to procure the assistance of the Government in the establishment of the school, there was sufficient public spirit in the community to build and equip an institution fully equal to any county Grammar School in the country, outside of two or three of the large cities. It is this spirit of personal effort and personal sacrifice in the public interest that we desire to commemorate, and, if possible, perpetuate—a spirit that is the parent of all true progress, and without which no system, however well designed or elaborate, can produce results fully satisfactory.

Soon after the failure, or partial failure, of the effort made in 1843, for it is not probable that the intention to establish a Grammar School, in pursuance of the Act of 1841, was altogether abandoned, a new actor appeared on the scene that materially changed the aspect of affairs. Mr. John A. Carman, the youngest of eight sons of Michael Carman, was born in 1810. At the age of sixteen he was apprenticed to the harness business in Prescott. Subsequently he carried on the business in Prescott, and later in Brockville and Cornwall, until failing health compelled him to abandon it and spend a few years in a milder climate. During his enforced retirement he travelled over a considerable portion of the United States, and, no doubt, made himself familiar with the American school system. About 1844, he returned to his native place, and finding that the canals were being built, and the outlook for the future improving, he decided to make this his permanent home. But he felt that it lacked one thing more than any other—that was, the means of providing a more liberal education to the youth of the neighborhood and surrounding country. This he determined, as far as in him lay, to correct, by the erection of a suitable building. He had no land of his own except a lot that he had just purchased from Mr. James Coons, and on which he was about erecting a building to be used as a general store; but Messrs. James and Matthew Coons, sons of the Jacob Coons who, in 1786, had drawn the east half of Lot 23, now owned both the east and west halves of that lot, on the front of which were the prospective locks, the mill privileges and the wharf.

These brothers, whose mother was a Carman, were strongly imbued with that zeal in the cause of religion and good morals that was so conspicuous a feature in the character of the principal promoters of this enterprise. Matthew built a stone wall or fence in front of his yard or lawn, on the outside of which, appeared in very large Roman letters, made of stones of another color, the one word

TEMPERANCE.

His brother James, with equal zeal but less prudence, put a stipulation in the deed of every village lot he parted with, that no liquor should be sold on the premises. During the progress of the work on the Canal, this clause was violated by one or two parties, and he entered suit to enforce the agreement. He was successful in the lower courts, but the case was carried to Chancery, and "Jarndyce v. Jarndyce" was re-enacted on this side of the Atlantic, the cost being charged against the property. This continued until, wearied by delay and harrassed by creditors, Mr. Coons gathered up his few remaining belongings and left the country. The farm was subsequently sold by the sheriff to pay the costs.

They saw, however, the advantages that would result from the establishment of a first-rate school, and promptly acceded to Mr. Carman's proposal to give the land if he would erect the building, and made over to him one acre, lying about three hundred feet north of the front road. On this the building was erected during the summer of 1845. It is described in a letter from Mr. Carman to Dr. Bond, of New York, written on the 29th of November of that year, and as this letter not only describes the building but gives Mr. Carman's reasons for erecting it, in his own words, and is further illustrative of the conditions that prevailed, and the views that were held at the time, we give it in full.

MATILDA, EASTERN DISTRICT, C. W.,
DR. BOND, *November 29th*, 1845.

DEAR SIR,—Having been a reader of the *Christian Advocate and Journal* for a few years past, and observing your reports of visits to Colleges, Academies, Seminaries and the various Conferences, I am satisfied to confide in you as a competent and desirable judge of what I am now in immediate want of, *i.e.*, a competent person to take charge of a seminary, now new and in way of finishing. It is situate on the bank of the St. Lawrence, fourteen miles east of Ogdensburg, within fifty rods of the mail steamers' landing in Canada. Building is 57 x 32 feet, two storeys, stone, divided into twelve rooms: one dining, one kitchen, one sitting, and two bedrooms for family department; one large school-room, twenty-nine feet square, seated and ventilated on the plans of a book entitled, "Schools and Schoolmasters": one room twenty-two feet square, and one large teachers' or recitation room. The remaining four rooms were for boarders. I have been thus explicit, in order that time may be saved in making enquiry, and I would state still further the Township is generally well settled, and Methodist is the leading or most popular denomination of Christians in the neighborhood, a chapel within one mile. The canal, now in progress, is building a lock and mill privilege just at the steamboat landing.

The deficiency of the like places of education in these parts has compelled many of our best farmers and merchants to send their children to the neighboring State to be educated. This, together with the present move by our Legislature, have made impressions on my mind which have led to the erecting of this building. I may here acquaint you with the fact that I am the sole and entire proprietor. Two of my neighbors have, however, granted half an acre each to the building. I will also just here remark, I never expect any return of capital, but trust it will pay its way. I, however, think it preferable to obtain a teacher of British or Canadian birth. It would do away with prejudices in some; and in case the moneys now offered for Grammar Schools can be obtained without affecting the government of the school, such a person will be desirable. And now as to the teacher's qualifications, I will entirely submit it to your well-informed judgment, only that he be a person of character, deep piety, capable of lecturing on the various sciences usually taught in such seminaries. I anticipate, should approved teachers be obtained, male and female, that one hundred and twenty or thirty scholars may be obtained. I do not expect over fifty or sixty to commence with, unless some public display of notices be made. I am not fully prepared to say how I would prefer starting

OLD GRAMMAR SCHOOL.

the institution. I would either rent the building on most moderate terms, hire the teachers myself, or put it in the hands of a Board of Managers—any way that will be most agreeable and advisable. Should the principal teacher, which you would recommend, prefer taking the family department, and board the pupils that should offer as boarders, to the number of eight or ten, he can do so, and the salary, in addition to that privilege, will be from $400 to $500 per annum; of course, paying according to abilities.

And now I am through with what I thought proper to communicate in order that a correct opinion may be formed before an answer could be at all fully given by the person you should recommend, and I hope you will not think this communication presumptuous and too troublesome. I confess it is a stretch of propriety in me thus to address an entire stranger. My only excuse is, we are all but entirely deficient in competent persons of the right, improved system of teaching, and if you will take an interest in our prosperity in this respect, you will, no doubt, meet a reward, if not in this life, in the life to come. I think of but two or three persons to whom I can refer them to in New York city, *i.e.*, Mr. Freeland, of the firm of Eli & Freeland, corner of William and Cedar Streets; Moses Maynard, Banker, and George Weir, in the Custom House.

J. A. CARMAN.

Mr. Carman evidently found it difficult to obtain a suitable person to take charge of the school, for we find him during the winter corresponding with other parties to the same purport; and, on the 9th of March, 1846, he wrote Bishop Alley, of the American Methodist Episcopal Church, telling him that he had thus far been unsuccessful, and asking his assistance. He had now, however, decided what he would do with the property, for he says in this letter that he has appointed seven persons, including himself, as trustees, of what he says he may now term "our Grammar School, in accordance with our Act;" and adds, speaking of the prospective teacher, "I may now more distinctly remark, he must be of British or colonial birth."

The deed, which was executed on the 1st of April, 1846, is from James Coons and wife to George Brouse, Jacob Brouse, Philip Carman, and John A. Carman, of Matilda; and J. W. Rose, John P. Crysler, and Wm. Sharts, of Williamsburg, and their successors in office. The consideration is nominal (one pound five shillings), and there are no special conditions in the deed. It will be observed that Mr. Carman had previously said that he was the owner, and that James and Matthew Coons had each given half the land. No doubt some arrangement had been made, giving Mr. Carman the property before the building was erected, which had probably never been registered; and when it was decided to deed to Trustees, of whom he was one, it was thought best to have the deed come direct from Mr. Coons. The land formed the centre of a square of eight lots—four front and four rear; the four front ones facing on what is now College Street. The deed covered the four centre lots of this square, two front and two rear, five-sixths of which were on Mr. James Coons' land.

The Trustees were chosen from the first men in the county; all of them except the two Carmans and the Rev. Wm. Sharts being at the time aspirants for parliamentary honors.

George Brouse owned a large farm just east of the Coons' property, was a lumber merchant, kept a store and the post-office, and nearly twenty years before had been elected to the Legislative Assembly of Upper Canada; and, as late as 1857, was again a candidate. He was one of the principal promoters of the incorporation of the village in 1857, and was its first Reeve.

Jacob Brouse, who lived about one mile west of the village, was also an extensive farmer and merchant; and, at the time he was appointed Trustee, was a leading member of the District Council, and in 1853 became Warden of the Counties. Though comparatively unlettered, he was a man of considerable ability, and a warm friend of education.

John P. Crysler was the son of Colonel John Crysler, who had represented the county from 1808 to 1824; and was himself elected in 1848, and again in 1854.

J. W. Rose was also a member of one of the old county families, was a man of great force of character, a fluent speaker, and the hope and pride of his political friends in the county. He defeated Mr. Crysler in 1851, and represented

GEORGE BROUSE.   JACOB BROUSE.
PHILIP CARMAN.   J. W. ROSE.

the county three years, but was in turn defeated in 1854. Rev. Wm. Sharts was minister in charge of the Lutheran congregation in Williamsburg.

Philip Carman was the elder brother of Mr. John A. Carman. He had received, or rather acquired, a better education than any of his colleagues, except, perhaps, the Rev. Wm. Sharts; was cool, urbane, and very methodical, and possessed unusual skill in framing and arranging legal documents. His limited means prevented him from seeking parliamentary position, but he was one of the best equipped public men of his time; was the first Clerk and principal organizer of the Matilda Township Council, was for many years Reeve of his native village, and in his turn Warden of the Counties.

The four Matilda representatives and Mr. Rose were Methodists; Mr. Crysler and, of course, Mr. Sharts were Lutherans. Mr. Sharts, we assume, was not a politician; Mr. George Brouse and Mr. Crysler were Conservatives, while the remaining four members were Liberals.

Mr. Crysler and Mr. Sharts were doubtless selected as representatives of what might be termed outside interests, but their influence on the school proved very slight; the four Matilda men and Mr. Rose, who had married a daughter of Peter Shaver, Esq., and was a brother-in-law of Mr. Philip Carman, practically forming the Board.

CHAPTER IV.

First School—Engaging the Principal—The Curriculum—Fees—Mr. Gates—Miss Bailey—Mr. Truax—School Diaries—Visitors—First Pupils.

THE new Board organized by appointing Mr. Jacob Brouse, Chairman, and Mr. Philip Carman, Secretary. The building was supplied with the necessary desks, painted and ready for use, when handed over by Mr. Carman. About all that was required in the way of furnishings to carry out the original design was a piano. This was purchased in Montreal, the price paid being $180; of this $50 was paid by J. W. Rose, $50 by George Brouse, and $50 by J. A. Carman; the remaining $30 appears to have been paid by Jacob Brouse. The piano was delivered and in the building before the School was opened.

Mr. J. A. Carman had traversed the continent for a teacher without success, perhaps because his ideal was higher than the probable revenues of the School warranted; perhaps because we are inclined to look far afield when what we really need may be at our hand. At all events the Trustees secured as teacher a Mr. H. N. Gates, B.A., a divinity student, whose family, though American, lived in the adjoining Township of Edwardsburg. He may have possessed all the gifts and acquirements sought for in a teacher, but he was not British-born, and, consequently, could not at once procure the necessary authorization to teach a Grammar School in Canada. It is probably due to this cause that we have no record of the School during the first term (or quarter) except the payment of the salary in the yearly account.

The School opened on the 10th of June, 1846, without any definite agreement as to terms, for, on the 7th of August, we find Mr. Gates, who must then have been teaching, making the following propositions to the Trustees:

"Having considered the requirements, conditions and cir-
"cumstances attendant on the taking charge of your institu-
"tion as Principal, and being aware that in part, at present, I
"am unable to fulfil the requirements, in consequence of not
"being a British subject, I propose to take the charge of it on
"the following conditions:

"1. Should I within three months become qualified as the
"law requires, and should the annual income of the institu-
"tion amount to the sum of one hundred and seventy-five
"pounds, then that I shall receive as my salary the sum of
"one hundred and twelve pounds, ten shillings, together with
"the use of the family department of the building.

"2. Should I fail to become qualified as the law directs,
"and still the apportionment of the Government Grant now
"in reserve for the use of this institution be secured for its
"benefit, then I engage to receive the tuition of the pupils as
"my compensation during the first term.

"3. Should I not become qualified as the law directs, and,
"in consequence thereof, the apportionment of the Govern-
"ment Grant be lost to the institution, then I agree to demand
"no compensation for my services during the first term.

"4. Should I become qualified as above stated, and the
"annual income of the institution from all sources be less
"than one hundred and seventy-five pounds, then that I
"receive one hundred pounds and the use of the family
"department of the building as compensation for my services.

"5. I agree to provide a teacher for the female department
"while I remain in charge of the institution, at the rate of
"fifty pounds a year.

"6. Should either of the parties concerned in the above
"propositions become dissatisfied, they shall be annulled by
"notice given by the dissatisfied party at least six weeks
"before the close of any regular term of the School."

The first proposition appears to have been finally acceded to by the Trustees, and Mr. Gates was no doubt successful in overcoming the disqualification; though it seems probable that at the close of 1846 the school had not an assured income of £175 per annum, as the accounts show but £50 as the half-year's salary of the Principal, and £25 as that of the assistant. It is evident, however, that the prospect brightened during the winter, as, at the close of the next half-year, he received the £56 5s., and £6 5s. as arrears.

In September, 1846, the Trustees made a vigorous effort to "boom" their new school by issuing handbills or posters setting forth its advantages. One of these has been preserved. From it we learn that Mr. H. N. Gates, B.A., was the principal; Miss Sarah A. Bailey, assistant; and one John L. Truax, music teacher. The general advantages of the institution and its situation are then set forth, and the terms of tuition given. For the common English branches—spelling, reading, writing, arithmetic, grammar, history and geography—the charge is fifteen shillings for term of eleven weeks. For the higher branches—algebra, astronomy, geometry, trigonometry, book-keeping, rhetoric, logic, botany, geology, chemistry, natural philosophy and natural theology—the charge is one pound for a similar term; and for the languages—Latin, Greek, German and French—one pound five shillings. For drawing, five shillings extra was charged; for painting, ten shillings; and for music, one pound ten shillings; and five shillings for the use of the piano.

Complaint is frequently made that the subjects now taught in our High Schools are too numerous: but this curriculum, especially when it is understood that natural philosophy includes the whole range of physical science, is all-embracing enough for the most fully equipped of our modern institutions. The difference appears to be that most of the subjects at present taught in our schools are obligatory, and that the teachers, under the eye of the ubiquitous inspector, must be able to cover the whole ground, while fifty years ago the students might select such branches of study as they desired to pursue, it being understood that they would be guided somewhat by the advice of their teachers, who would, naturally enough, direct them in paths most familiar to themselves.

Of the teachers thus advertised, we know but little of Mr. Gates, except that he appears to have taught with acceptance for a year and a half.

Miss Sarah A. Bailey was of an old Puritan family, and the daughter of Judge Bailey, of Potsdam, N.Y. She was eminently successful as a teacher, and soon won her way to the hearts of her pupils, but her intercourse with the trustees appears to have led to the winning of another heart and the making of another engagement, and she and Mr. John A. Carman, who had up to this time been a bachelor, were married in the early part of 1850.

Mr. Truax seems to have been a sort of wandering minstrel. We have not been able to learn whence he came or whither he went, nor, in fact, anything about him, further than that he was blind and that he taught music for a time in the "Seminary."

During the fall term of 1846, which might be said to be the first regular term of the school, diaries were kept by each pupil (of course under direction of the teacher), descriptive of his conduct in school, and the progress made in his studies each day. The pupil got credit, first, for "Conduct": second, for "Diligence," and then followed the several studies he was pursuing, such as Grammar, Geography, Latin—four in each line—that is, four for "Conduct," four for "Diligence," four for Grammar, etc., was the highest number of marks given. Each page covers a week's work, and it is signed at the bottom by the teacher and the parent. It is interesting to note the conduct and progress of the young man at school in the light of his subsequent career.

Several of the students, among them Hiram R. Haines, Reuben Hickey and Ormond Skinner, are nearly perfect: William and Philip Keeler, Rufus Carman and James Ault, also stand high; Alonzo Bowen, Guy C. Ault, Guy Brouse and Cyrus Brouse, show considerable falling off, but the worst one in the lot is Albert Carman, the future principal of the school and of Albert College, and the present head of the Methodist Church in Canada. One week, on Monday, he made one mark in Grammar; on Tuesday and Wednesday, no mark at all; on Thursday, one mark in Geography; on Friday, two in Grammar, and on Saturday, one in Geography, while perfect marks for him would have been twenty-eight each day. Well might his father write at the bottom of the page before signing it, "This week seems a blank." Yet, of all the students then in the school, or for that matter, all who have since been in it, none has been a more distinguished success in life than the maker of this inferior record. His history is a rather striking example of what industry, perseverance and singleness of purpose can accomplish.

Fifty years ago it was customary to have visitors of schools, and, at least until the Local Superintendents and Inspectors took their places, clergymen, magistrates, and, we believe, some other members of the community were recognized by law as Visitors of our common or public schools. Among the first of the acts performed by the Trustees of this school was the appointment of Visitors. These were, so far as we have been able to ascertain, Rev. E. J. Boswell, John Archibald, Rev. John Lever, Rev. Bishop Alley, Peter Shaver, William Patrick, and James West, Esquires. The duties of the Visitors were not onerous. They were expected to take an interest in the school, to attend examinations, if convenient, and call occasionally when in the neighborhood. On the other hand, the association of the school with the names of men eminent or prominent, was supposed to give tone and character to the institution, and to be a warrant to the public that it was worthy of patronage and support.

The school appears to have reached the high-water mark of its early days in the winter term of 1847, when thirty-eight male and twenty-five female students were in attendance. They were almost exclusively the children of wealthy parents, and were principally from the front of Matilda and Williamsburg, though there were a few from Oznabruck and Edwards-

SEMI-CENTENNIAL OF IROQUOIS HIGH SCHOOL. 31

burg, and one or two from Kemptville and Prescott. They confined their studies largely to the common English branches, though nearly half the school aimed higher. There was a Latin class of six, James Ault, Cyrus Brouse, Albert Carman, Philip Keeler, N. Knapp and Ormond Skinner, while just one, James Ault, took French. Three, Mary Brouse, A. Gates, and Elizabeth Wylie, took music. Only one, Mr. L. Pillar, devoted himself to Painting, while the Drawing class numbered seventeen, Messrs. Cyrus Brouse, J. Cook, Rufus Carman, R. Hickey, D. S. Hickey, Wm. Keeler and J. Mills ; Misses Nancy Brouse, M. Brouse, Uretta Coons, Emily Coons, A. Lever, M. McIlmoyle, A. Mills, Charlotte Parlow, Elizabeth and Annie Wylie. Trigonometry claimed the attention of but three pupils, Philip Keeler, N. Knapp, and John Suffel. Geometry, one, N. Knapp. Algebra, eight, James Ault, Cyrus Brouse, H. J. Cook, Albert Carman, R. Hickey, Wm. Keeler, J. S. Rattray and John Suffel. Six devoted their attention to Astronomy, Cyrus Brouse, H. J. Cook, R. Hickey, Wm. Keeler; Misses McIlmoyle and Elizabeth Wylie. The Philosophy class was larger, consisting of Messrs. James Ault, Cyrus Brouse, H. J. Cook, R. Hickey, Wm. Keeler, J. S. Rattray, Colin Rose, Ormond Skinner; Misses Uretta Coons, A. Gates, M. McIlmoyle, M. Steacy, Elizabeth and Annie Wylie—fourteen. Three appeared to have studied Logic, S. Ault, H. J. Cook, and N. Knapp, and the same number Chemistry, E. Gates, J. S. Rattray, and O. Skinner. Nine devoted themselves to History, thirty-six to Geography, fifty-six to Arithmetic, fifty-three to Grammar, fifty-seven to Reading, forty to Writing, and thirty to Spelling. The names of the pupils who confined themselves to the common branches were : Guy C. Ault, Guy Brouse, Alonzo Bowen, B. Coons, G. Cook, N. Coons, William and Robert Elliot, W. H. Fraser, H. Haines, E. Keeler, S. Robertson, J. G. Skinner, Joseph Skinner, E. Selleck, L. O. Soules, James Wylie, Jas. Wood, A. Dixon, John Parlow, Charlotte Ault, J. Ault, J. Bowen, Mary Carman, Maria Carman, Emma Carman, F. Carman, M. Carman, M. A. Coons, C. M. Ross, H. Steacy, A. Steacy—thirty-two.

CHAPTER V.

Mr. Dick—Examinations—How Teachers were Appointed—Condition of the County—Prizes—County and Local Boards of Trustees—New School Law—William Elliot—Robert Lowery—Ryerson's Visit—Public Library Established.

R. GATES resigned at the close of 1847, and was succeeded by the Rev. A. Dick, a Baptist minister. His letter of acceptance is dated at a place called Ramsayville, and in it he suggests that, if he can procure a suitable domestic to take the care of his little daughter, Mrs. Dick may become his assistant in the school, as she is "acquainted with needle-work, painting, botany, French, etc." His residence does not appear to have been a great distance from the school, as he promises, if the sleighing be good, to be here on the first Tuesday in January. He did not, however, reach the school until about a week later.

There were no general certificates at that time, but every teacher or person who desired to teach was expected to present himself to the District Board for examination. This Mr. Dick did on the 3rd of February following, and the result is indicated in the following letter:

CORNWALL, *3rd February*, 1848.
MR. PHILIP CARMAN,
SIR,—The Rev. Alexander Dick presented himself this day for examination before the Board of Trustees, and I have the pleasure to inform you that the result of his examination has proved satisfactory.
You must understand, however, that the approval of Mr. Dick's appointment rests with the Governor-General.

Mr. Dick will be nominated and proposed for His Excellency's approval as soon as the Trustees have received certain testimonials from Mr. Dick, which are deemed of importance.

I have the honor to be, Sir,

Your most obedient servant,

H. URQUHART, *Chairman.*

Rev. Hugh Urquhart was a Presbyterian minister, an old teacher in the Cornwall Grammar School, and an educationist of considerable repute. He was understood at the time to have formed a high estimate of Mr. Dick's attainments, especially in Greek. Everything appeared to promise well for the school. The first year Mr. Dick was in it the Government grant, which had been but thirty, was raised to ninety pounds; the attendance was good, the fame of the school was extending; yet, as will be seen hereafter, the seeds of future trouble had already been planted by the manner of his appointment, as indicated in Mr. Urquhart's letter.

Yet for two or three years everything appeared to go on swimmingly. Soon the students from this school began to take the places of the Old Country and American teachers that had hitherto supplied the wants of the common schools. In 1850 Local Superintendents were first appointed, and Mr. Dick was placed over all the schools in Matilda. The Superintendents within the county formed an Examining Board for common school teachers. At the meetings of this board the pupils from this school acquitted themselves creditably, and it soon became recognized as a nursery for teachers within the county.

Just about this time other important changes were taking place in the conditions of the surrounding country. Hitherto the principal articles of export, and the means of making money, were either timber, wood or potash in some of its forms. The trade in these was almost entirely controlled by the farmer merchants, who lived along the river, the surplus products of the farms being principally used to supply the lumbermen or cordwood drawers, and to pay store bills. But the continual attacks on the woods had produced large clearings; these were increased in size by extensive fires that, about that time, ran over the imperfectly cleared parts of the county. Large areas well adapted to the growth of wheat and barley were brought under cultivation, and the district was rapidly transformed from a lumbering to a grain-growing and grain-exporting section of country. At the same time the Municipal Act, nearly as we have it now, became operative: and, in 1850, the first Township Council was elected. This stirred the farmers in the rear, many of whom were becoming wealthy, to seek representative positions, and a sort of levelling-up process began. The line between the front and rear became less marked; not that the front receded, but rather that the rear progressed more rapidly. Nor were the friends of the school slow to take advantage of these favoring conditions, as the following extract from the *Journal of Education* for April, 1850, makes manifest:

"John A. Carman, Esq., the munificent founder of the Dundas Seminary in Matilda, has written to the Rev. A. Dick, Superintendent of Common Schools for that Township, stating that he will place in that gentleman's hands next January a prize of £12 10s., to be awarded as follows: To the teacher of the best and most efficiently managed school in the Township, £5; to the Trustees of the same, in apparatus, £2; to the teacher of the second best school, £4; to the Trustees of the same, £1. 10s. The time which said teachers shall have taught in this Township in the year 1850 shall not be less than eight months; and the Trustees shall not be entitled to the award unless their school has been taught six months in the year 1850 by the teacher who may receive the award. The prize to be annual, provided the experiment proves satisfactory. George Brouse, Esq., has also promised a similar prize on the same conditions. William Elliot, Esq , has further pledged himself to give a prize of the same amount to the writer of the best essay (who must be a Teacher in the Township) on 'The Most Effective and Best Method of Teaching Common Schools.' In communicating these encouragements to exertion to the Trustees and teachers of the Township, Mr. Dick adds, 'You will also receive the *Journal of Education* for the present year through the liberality of Jacob Brouse, Esq., Town Reeve, and George Brouse, Esq., Councillor. It will remain the property of the several school sections, each receiving one number monthly, and ought to be preserved. You may expect a visit and lecture from me in the month of July.' At the close of the gratifying examination of the Dundas Grammar

School, of which Mr. Dick is Principal, Mr. Albert Carman, a pupil, delivered a very eloquent address on 'Education,' which has been published."

Whether the prizes offered were duly competed for and won, does not appear; but it is evident that there was a great deal of interest being taken in education, and that the school was not only regarded as being in a flourishing condition, but that the Principal had thus far won the approval of the Trustees. Unfortunately this was not to continue. We have seen that Grammar School teachers were at that time appointed by the Governor-General, on recommendation of the District Grammar School Trustees; and that though the Local Board, appointed by Mr. Carman, controlled the school property, they were not recognized by law as Grammar School Trustees. They had hired Mr. Dick, but in order to draw the Government grant, it had been necessary to procure an appointment from the Governor, in the prescribed way. This made him Grammar School teacher for the county, and in a measure independent of the Local Board, as they could not remove him from his position, though they might eject him from the school building. This divided authority, as might be expected, resulted in friction between the Trustees and teacher, and seriously menaced the prospects of the institution.

The situation is well described in the following letter from Messrs. Geo. Brouse and Philip Carman to Dr. Ryerson, written nearly two years later, or, on the 6th February, 1852:

"We hold a deed of trust of one of the best and most extensive buildings in Canada West erected for school purposes in a country place. The building was erected by Mr. J. A. Carman, of this place, entirely at his own expense; the land in connection with it was given by Messrs. Matthew and James Coons, and all was freely given into our hands for the public good as a Board of Local Trustees in May, 1846, and on the 10th day of June the same year we opened a school in the building under the superintendence of Mr. H. N. Gates. At the time the school opened it was not legally a Grammar School. Subsequently, however, Mr. Gates passed through the regular course and obtained his certificate, and our school was recognized as one of the additional Grammar Schools for the District. At the close of 1847, Mr. Gates resigned, and was succeeded by the Rev. A. Dick (Baptist) as Principal, who has been in charge since. At this time ('47) the Government grant was £25 or £30; in '48 it was raised to over £90. This, or something else, had a bad tendency; the teacher did not give the satisfaction he had formerly done. The consequence is, that now for the last year the attendance has been from 15 to 30 (in '47 it was as large as 70). We are anxious for a change, but are unable to effect it, as the teacher under the present system is beyond our control. He is aware that we are anxious for his removal, but he has given us to understand that he is not beholden to us, or to be controlled by us; that if we turn him out of our building he is still the teacher of the Dundas Grammar School, and that he would only have to remove to some other locality and procure a building, and thus deprive us of the Grammar School, after all that has been done to establish it here.

"We are decidedly of the opinion that the law wants amending, so as to place a part of the control into the hands of a Local Board of Trustees, who certainly are most interested in the prosperity of the school, so far at least as hiring and discharging the teacher, subject, of course, to his procuring the necessary certificate of qualification, and such other restrictions as may be deemed necessary. As the law now stands, and the Government grant being considerable, it makes the teachers independent of other support, and they become careless and indolent, and, in too many cases we fear, intemperate. We should feel ourselves deeply indebted to you, if your time would permit you, to look into the system and provide a remedy."

Dr. Ryerson's reply, dated 10th February, reads:

"GENTLEMEN,—I have the honor to acknowledge the receipt of yours of the 6th inst., and to state in reply that I concur in the views which you express in regard to the management of Grammar Schools. In 1850, at the request of the then Attorney-General, I prepared a draft of a Grammar School Bill, which provided, among other things, for the appointment of Grammar School Trustees by County Councils, and the appointment and removal of masters of the Grammar Schools by the Trustees thus appointed, but the bill, though introduced by Mr. Hincks, was laid over. I think, however, the subject will be taken up again at the ensuing session of our Legislature."

Dr. Ryerson was as good as his word; soon after this the Act of 1853 (16 Vic.) was passed. It authorized the appointment of not less than six nor more than eight Trustees for each Grammar School, with the powers asked for in the letter of Messrs. Brouse and Carman; and, at a special meeting of the Counties Council, at Cornwall, on January 6th, 1854, just before the expiration of the term of the members elected in 1853, Messrs. Wm. Elliot, Philip Carman, and Robert Lowery, were appointed. The new Board appears to have consisted of these three gentlemen and Jacob Brouse, J. W. Rose, and Walter Bell, though I have been unable to ascertain when or how the three last-named were appointed.

It will be seen the new Board consisted of three members of the old Board, Messrs. Carman, Rose, and Brouse, and three new members, Messrs. Elliot, Lowery, and Bell.

Mr. Elliot was a Scotchman, born in the last year of the last century. He came to America when a young man, spent some years in New York State and in Canada East, and subsequently started business as a brewer at Mille Roches. While there he secured a contract on the canal here—moved to Matilda, married Miss Emma Bowen, a niece of Mr. Carman, and thenceforth made this village his home. The contract proved a profitable one; and, when the canal was completed, he leased the best milling privilege, built a large flouring mill, and for many years carried on an extensive business. He was a man of considerable public spirit, served some time as Councillor in the township and Reeve of the village after its incorporation, and, in 1858, became Warden of the Counties. Like most Scotchmen, he placed a high value on education, was a staunch friend of the School, and did much to promote its interests. He died in 1891, in his ninety-second year.

Robert Lowery was a young and very ambitious Irishman, born about 1820; he came to this country with his father, John Lowery, when a boy. His early years were devoted to assisting his father to clear up a farm in the Township of Matilda, and to executing some small contracts on the Williamsburg Canal. About, or a little before, 1850, he bought a saw-mill at what is now Hainsville, in the township of Matilda, and a little later went into mercantile business at Dixon's Corners. He was one of the first Municipal Councillors of the Township; was Reeve in 1852, Deputy-Reeve in 1853, '55, '56 and '64, and continued in the Council until failing health compelled him to retire in 1865. In 1863 he unsuccessfully contested the county with Mr Ross. His native abilities were of a high order, though his opportunities for their cultivation had been limited. He was a good debater, with the glib tongue of an Irishman, ready in repartee, and strong in invective. In the unsparing use of the latter he frequently provoked hostility; he had warm friends and bitter enemies.

Walter Bell was a leading business man at North Williamsburg; was Reeve of the Township of Williamsburg for several years, beginning in 1850; but it does not appear that he ever took much interest in the affairs of the school.

There were now two Boards of Trustees; the one held the school property by deed from John A. Carman, while in the other was vested the control of the school. Steps were, however, at once taken to place everything with the Trustees appointed under the new School Act, and on the 30th August, 1854, an agreement was concluded whereby they leased the school property for a term of five years at a rental of £12 10s. a year, payable half-yearly. Whether the rent was ever paid we have no means of knowing, but it is probable that it was merely nominal, or, at most, as a sort of bond or security that the property would be devoted to the purposes originally contemplated.

Another event of considerable importance, educationally, occurred during the last year of Mr. Dick's incumbency. The School Act of 1850 had made provision for the establishment of public libraries in Townships. Early in the year 1853, Dr. Ryerson, the Chief Superintendent of Education, visited the county, and held a meeting in the Grammar School; Jacob Brouse, who was Warden that year, presiding.

The Doctor's mission was to urge the adoption of the Free School system and the establishment of public libraries. The meeting was not large, but the discussion, in which George Brouse, Philip Carman, Edmund Doran, Wm. Elliot, J. S.

Ross and some others took part, was interesting. It was explained that arrangements had been made whereby the books could be got cheaply; that the Government would supplement every dollar provided by the local municipality with another dollar; and that thus a very valuable library could be procured at slight expense to the ratepayers. Jacob Brouse was the Reeve; and Messrs. Elliot, Ross, Lowery, and Simon Strader Councillors. The matter was taken up at a meeting of the Council held subsequently; a grant of £100 proposed and finally carried, Messrs. Lowery and Strader voting nay.

The result was the establishment of a first-class library for the Township, containing about 1,000 volumes. There was a Township Librarian appointed, and each School Section appointed a Section Librarian. The business of the Township Librarian was to distribute to the School Section Librarians, who in turn distributed among the people. The system was perhaps too elaborate for the circumstances and the time, and lacked a permanent inspectoral head to enforce the regulations. The librarians, even the Township Librarian, were frequently changed, and were sometimes inefficient. The books got scattered, and it was hard, impossible, in fact, to get them in again; the movement had never been a popular one with the majority of the ratepayers, and no means were taken by succeeding Councils to replace lost volumes; besides, the incorporation of the village in 1857 split the collection, and withdrew some influences from the Township that would have been favorable to its maintenance.

The outcome was, that twenty years after its establishment, there ceased to be a Township or Village Library. Nevertheless, in many homes in both Township and village, some of these books may yet be found; the seed was sown; and though some, perhaps much, of it fell by the wayside, if we could trace its influence on the lives, the character, and the achievements of those among whom it was scattered, we would find that enough fell on good ground to amply justify the effort that had been put forth.

CHAPTER VI.

Albert Carman—General Prosperity—James Croil—J. S. Ross—Effect of their Appointment—Protracted Meeting—Disciplining a Student—The Methodist Church—Belleville Seminary—Retirement of Mr. Carman.

HE fortunes of the school were never perhaps at a lower ebb than in the early part of 1854. As has been seen, Mr. Dick and the Trustees were not in harmony; and Mrs. Dick, it appears, had not proved a success as an assistant; but the new Board, composed of local men, tried friends of the institution, were now in full control, and the prospect soon brightened.

Mr. Albert Carman, eldest son of Philip Carman, the not too promising pupil of 1847, the youth of 1850 whose essay had been thought worthy of publication, had just graduated from Victoria College; and was chosen by the Board to succeed Mr. Dick. He had barely reached his majority, and had never had any experience in teaching; but he was at once capable, earnest, and unpretending; and early won the esteem and love of his pupils. He had the charm of youth and commanded the respect—almost the veneration—that we usually accord only to those of much riper years.

The times were also propitious. The Grand Trunk Railway was being built; the commencement of the Crimean War had closed the Baltic and Black Sea ports, from which Great Britain had hitherto drawn a large proportion of her food supply, so that the demand for wheat from America was enormously increased; while the mines of California and

WILLIAM ELLIOT.
JOHN S. ROSS.　A. B. SHERMAN, M.D.　JAMES CROIL.
ROBERT LOWERY.

Australia were adding at an unprecedented rate to the world's stock of gold. These conditions, present at the same time, caused a rise in prices of farm products, and an appreciation of land values, that created an abounding prosperity, in which the people of this County fully shared. The one dark spot in this, so far as this village was concerned, was that there was no road leading north into the country farther than the Third Concession until you went a mile east; while the neighboring village of Morrisburg was more fortunately situated in this respect, and was thus enabled to secure the lion's share of the produce trade. The activity of trade and the demand for labor naturally opened up other avenues of advancement for the young, and may have tended to draw attention from the institution: but there is no doubt that it, to some extent, shared in the general prosperity, though the records of the school for the first year and a half, or while it may be said to have been passing from the old Board to the new, do not appear to have been preserved.

In 1856 two new members were appointed to places on the Board, who exercised a marked influence on the school for several years : and one of whom served longer than any other member except, perhaps, Mr. Philip Carman. These were James Croil and J. S. Ross.

Mr. Croil was a Scotchman, who about the middle of the century purchased and settled on the Crysler Farm, so famed on account of the battle fought there in 1813. He was a gentleman of culture and means, and devoted a considerable portion of his time to literary pursuits; his work generally being in connection with, and for the benefit of, the Presbyterian Church, of which he was a member. He found time also to write a history of this county, known as "Croil's Dundas," a work of very great merit, the value of which increases as time goes on. He served on the Board ten years, during five of which, or from 1859 to the close of '62, and again in '65, he was chairman.

Mr. John Sylvester Ross was the son of an U.E. Loyalist, and was born in the Township of Oznabruck in 1821. He came to this place while the work on the canal was in progress, first as clerk and paymaster for Messrs. Geo. and Jas. Crawford, the contractors who built the locks. Soon after he opened a small store near the locks, married a daughter of Mr. Peter Carman, and settled here permanently. His energy and capacity for business soon gave him an assured position. About 1852, he became a member of the Township Council, and was Reeve in 1856. He was also a member of the Village Council for some time after its incorporation; and, probably, would have had his turn in the Reeve's chair only for a sort of unwritten law that—after Mr. George Brouse, who had got the first part of a year on account of his advanced years and his services in connection with the incorporation—no man not a Liberal in politics should be advanced to that position. He, however, got his compensation outside, for in 1861 he became the Parliamentary representative from the County and held the place, except during the six years, 1872-78, until his death in 1882. At the first meeting after his appointment to the Board he was chosen Secretary-Treasurer, and continued to serve in that capacity until 1866, when he became Chairman: after which, for nearly fourteen years, he presided at the meetings of the Board. He resigned in 1879.

Up to the time of the appointment of Messrs. Croil and Ross, the active managers of the school, with the single exception of Geo. Brouse, had been Reformers; and they had all been Methodists, until Mr. Elliot, a Presbyterian, was appointed in 1854. Not that they had been selected because of their political or religious views, but because theirs were the views that prevailed largely, almost universally, among the local promoters and friends of the institution. But, now that it had become a recognized County Grammar School, dependent, in some measure, on the Counties Council for support, and partially under the control of that body, which was composed largely, at least in this county, of adherents of the opposing political party; it was important that nothing should arise to create distrust of the management. Any danger of this was very much lessened, if not entirely obviated, by the cordial co-operation with the old members of the Board, of two prominent Conservatives, the one a Presbyterian and the other a member of the Church of England. It was an assurance to the public that in educational matters neither creed nor party was recognized.

Mr. Ross, who was the trusted leader of the Conservatives in the County during the whole period of his connection with the school, was, from his position, specially fitted to allay any irritation that might result from the friction of opposing views or interests. That he, to a great extent, succeeded in doing so, was subsequently made manifest by the almost entire absence of want of harmony between the village and Townships, in adjusting their respective contributions to the school.

The arrangement made in 1854, whereby the Trustees holding the deed leased to the county Trustees, was revised in 1856, and instructions given to prepare a new lease. This was for the full term of ninety-nine years from date, at a nominal rental of £1 per year. It was executed on the 12th day of June, 1857, and provided that the building should be kept insured, the institution being designated "Matilda County Grammar School."

In the spring of 1856, a wave of religious excitement swept over this part of the country. The Methodists, whose church had been up on "the Point," about half-a-mile from the centre of the village, had, in 1855, built a new and more commodious one on the site of the present one, erected twenty-one years later. This was dedicated in the early part of 1856, and a "protracted meeting," under the superintendence of the Rev. James Gray, followed. Night after night, for seven or eight weeks, the large edifice was crowded to the doors. Nearly every one in the village, and for miles beyond, was "converted" or under "conviction." Nothing approaching it had been witnessed since the great revival of 1823. The scenes in the church were impressive—sometimes appalling. Scores of men and women would be struggling in an agony of prayer, and shouting at the top of their voices for mercy, frequently falling on the floor, completely exhausted. No onlooker could fail to be moved. A few Presbyterians, members of the Church of England, and Roman Catholics, held aloof; but the great mass of the people, including nearly all the pupils in the Grammar School, joined the movement; or, as it was termed, "got religion."

One of the most promising students, a youth, whose conduct was otherwise irreproachable, not only refused to join, but was suspected of exerting an unfavorable influence on some fellow-students. He had a *penchant* for "pure science," and was said to have some books that were of very doubtful orthodoxy. The matter was brought to the attention of the trustees, and for some time his fate hung in the balance; but better counsels prevailed, and, instead of expelling him from the school, as had been proposed, the Chairman of the Board, Mr. Jacob Brouse, asked the assembled congregation to pray for him. That youth is now occupying the position on the Board then occupied by Mr. Brouse, and has for years exerted a considerable, frequently a prevailing, influence in its counsels. He still retains his love for science and its methods, but it is no longer regarded as inimical to the interests of the school.

At a meeting of the Board, held on the 5th of July, 1856, the salary of the headmaster was fixed at £150. There is no record of the salary allowed the assistant at this time; but, when Mr. Carman's successor was engaged, the lady who had been his last assistant, a Miss Ellsworth, was continued at £75 per year, she to devote sufficient time before and after school to give one music lesson each day.

The early Methodist missionaries, or preachers, in Canada were principally from the Methodist Episcopal Church of the United States. These were reinforced from time to time by helpers from England, and by local recruits, until a Canadian Conference was formed. About 1830, the question of the future relations of this Conference came up. Some were for continuing in connection with the American Church, and some for uniting with the Wesleyan body, in England. The views of the latter prevailed; the Old Country connection was established, and the Church became the Wesleyan Methodist Church of Canada. A remnant, consisting of some half-dozen clergymen and a considerable number of laymen, who remained true to their first love, refused to unite with the Wesleyans, and formed the Methodist Episcopal Church of Canada. Among these were the Carmans, of Matilda.

The new Church prospered; preachers were selected without any special qualification but their zeal and piety. Nevertheless, and perhaps for this very reason, they appeared to reach the hearts of the people among whom they labored; and the "Episcopals," as they were called, seemed likely soon to be able to dispute the supremacy with their Wesleyan brethren. What it was felt was needed most was a better educated clergy. To secure this, a school was being established in Belleville, which was at first called the "Belleville Seminary," but which in a few years acquired university powers, under the name of "Albert College."

Mr. Albert Carman was offered and accepted the professorship of mathematics in this school, which opened in July, 1857, and of which he became the Principal two years later. During the three years he was here steady progress had been made, and his leaving was deeply regretted by the pupils and friends of the Grammar School. His parting address was long remembered. He has since, as Bishop in the Methodist Episcopal Church, and later as head of the United Methodist Church in Canada, acquired continental fame as a speaker; but it is doubtful if he ever has found an audience so responsive as the little knot of students and friends who gathered around him on that day. It was no great oratorical effort; but every word that he said was so evidently from the heart, that it went straight to the hearts of those to whom it was addressed. The writer was there simply as a visitor, but, back through the mists of forty years, he can still hear the husky voice of the master and see the streaming eyes of the pupils as the affectionate words of counsel and advice and final leave-taking were being spoken.

CHAPTER VII.

Davies and Cowan—Changes in the School—Mr. Laing—Incorporation of the Village—Retirement of Mr. Davies—Mr. Cowan engaged—New Trustees—A. B. Sherman—Alex. McDonell—Dr. Worthington—Dr. Williams—Local Aid—*Laissez faire*—The Revenues—County Grants.

R. JACOB BROUSE, who had been Chairman almost continuously from the time the first Board was formed, retired permanently at the close of 1856; Mr. John A. Carman had done the same the previous year, and Messrs. Geo. Brouse and Rose some time earlier. Mr. Philip Carman alone of the original Trustees remained. He had acted as Secretary up to the time of Mr. Ross' appointment in 1856, he was Chairman in 1858, and retired from the Board at the close of 1860, but was reappointed in 1867, and was the Secretary and Treasurer from that time until the close of 1875. The Chairman who succeeded Mr. Brouse was the Rev. James Harris, a Church of England clergyman, at that time settled in Mountain. He remained but one year.

An event occurred in 1857, which, though not directly connected with the school, has been frequently referred to, and is, perhaps, of sufficient interest to warrant the giving to it a page or two here. Of all the stores that had been along the front road one only remained. It was about a mile east of the village, and near the front end of the main road, leading north through the centre of the Township. This road had been planked a few years before, and was the only outlet for the traffic that came to the village from the western part of

REV. DR. CARMAN,   DR. COWAN.
MRS. J. A. CARMAN,   MRS. W. C. BAILEY.

the county. The proprietor, John Laing, was a "brainy" and "peppery" little Scotchman, who had established a business there before there could be said to be a village here. He had a deservedly high reputation for honesty, Mr. George Brouse having said of him some time before, when a young man in his store, that he "would not be afraid to trust him with a drawerful of uncounted gold." He and Mr. Ross had commenced business about the same time, and there is no doubt regarded each other as rivals. They both sought and obtained seats at the Council Board of the Township. In 1856 Mr. Ross was Reeve, but, in 1857, Mr. Laing succeeded in getting two of the newly-elected members to support him, and thus secured the Reeveship and the control of the Council, as well as a place on the High School Board. In addition to the rivalry between the two gentlemen, there appears to have been a rivalry between the two school sections, No. 2, east of the village, and No. 3, in which the village was situated, and there was a farm or two, about midway between the school-houses, that was debatable ground. At the time this land was attached to the village section, but Mr. Laing, having a majority of the Council with him, got a by-law passed to detach it and unite it with his section, No. 2. This aroused the village, but as the Township was evidently with Mr. Laing, there was no remedy unless the village could be incorporated, and include this land within its limits. To do this in the ordinary way, through the Counties Council, required a population of 750, which was more than the place could then muster. There was no resource left but to apply to the Legislature for a special Act of Incorporation. This was done at once, the Act passed, and the new Council was elected in August. Mr. George Brouse was very active and influential in promoting the incorporation, and was elected Reeve for the balance of the year. His colleagues in the Council were : J. S. Ross, Wm. Elliot, Philip Carman and James Grier.

Though up to the time of incorporation the Post-office was officially known as Matilda, the village was frequently designated Cathcart, after the earl of that name, who commanded the British forces in Canada at the time of the resignation of Governor Sir Charles Metcalfe, in November, 1845, and who administered the Government until the arrival of Lord Elgin in January, 1847. The Point was known here and in the surrounding county as "Point Rockway"—a corruption of the Franco-Indian name, Iroquois, which appears to have been too much for our German ancestors. Even after it had been selected as the name of the village, and was frequently seen in print, it was a considerable time before even a majority of the people could get it right. And it is yet hard for some of us to drop the terminal letter. Perhaps we are still afield: to spell it phonetically, as we pronounce it, it would be ĭr-ŏ-kwóí, accenting the last syllable. It is not improbable that the French and Indians, from whom we received the name viva voce, accented the second syllable, making it ĭ-rŏk-woi, thus giving it when spoken rapidly, as French and Indians generally speak, the sound of "Rockway."

As an evidence of the haste with which the Act was hurried through the Legislature, though it was passed in the interest of the Common School here, the western part of the section, beyond the limit of the village, was left out in the cold, and it was necessary to get another Act passed the following year to attach it to the village for school purposes.

The incorporation of the village gave the ratepayers full control of their own taxes; and had the zeal for education manifested in 1843 and 1845 not waned a little, it would have been of advantage to this school; but other matters claimed the attention of the new Council. Streets were to be opened, sidewalks built, and roads improved, and it was not until some years later that the village, as a corporation, recognized its interest in the school, by contributing to its equipment or maintenance.

Mr. Carman's successor as master was a Mr. Edmund R. Davies. He came highly recommended; was an Englishman, a churchman, and, we believe, in politics a Tory. His attainments were said to be at least equal, if not superior, to those of any of his predecessors. He may have been, probably was, a very good man, but he was not a success here; he did not appear to be adapted to his environment. We remember hearing Mr. Laing, who was then a member of the School Board, say that there "was no use in anyone not a Methodist trying to teach this school." This was putting it unfairly, but there is no doubt that Mr. Davies failed to get in touch with the people or with the pupils. This is evidenced by the fact, that early in 1858 he applied to the Trustees for assistance in maintaining discipline. They stood by him in this, but it appears to have done no good, as in the following August his resignation, to take effect at the middle of the term, was tendered and accepted.

He is the only master that, so far as appears, ever asked for or received a testimonial from the Trustees. It reads:

"The Trustees of the Matilda County Grammar School hereby certify that Mr. Edmund R. Davies has taught this Grammar School for the last year, and they cheerfully bear testimony to his gentlemanly deportment and his general efficiency as a teacher, and have no hesitation in recommending him to the favorable consideration of any similar institution.

"Given under our hands at Iroquois, in the County of Dundas, the 19th August, 1858.

Signed,   "P. CARMAN, *Chairman.*
            "JAMES CROIL.
            "JOHN LAING.
            "J. S. ROSS, *Secretary.*"

At a subsequent meeting of the Trustees, Mr. Samuel Cowan was engaged as headmaster at the old salary, $600. Mr. Cowan was also an Englishman, but had come to this country when young, and was either a graduate or alumnus of Victoria College. He remained nearly a year and a half, or until the early part of 1860, when desiring to visit the old country, he asked to be relieved on condition that he furnish a substitute in Wm. A. Whitney, to complete the term ending June 22nd. The proposition was accepted by the Board. Mr. Cowan was fairly successful as a teacher, gave satisfaction to the Trustees, and might have remained longer had he so desired. After his return from England he graduated in medicine, married a daughter of Mr. Philip Carman, and about 1865 commenced the practice of his profession in Iroquois. In 1866 he was Secretary and Treasurer of the Grammar School Board. He appears to have been partial to the families of the old Trustees; for, having lost his first wife, he subsequently married her cousin, the daughter of Mr. Jesse W. Rose. He is now living in Wolfe Island, and has attained a good position in his profession.

The Trustees who served about this time not already noticed, were Dr. Sherman, Mr. Alex. McDonell, Dr. Worthington, and Dr. Williams.

Dr. A. B. Sherman was born in Vermont, kept a bookstore in Ogdensburg at the time of the Battle of Prescott, in 1838, subsequently graduated in medicine, and practised his profession in Waddington, N.Y. At that time we were not very well supplied with doctors, and he got frequent calls to this side. About 1850 he moved to Morrisburg, and soon had a large practice: he had considerable capacity for public business, and in 1859 was elected Reeve of Williamsburg, holding the position until 1867, when he became Warden of the Counties. In the year in which he was first elected Reeve, he became a member of the Grammar School Board, and thereafter for six years was among the most active and influential of its members: always exerting his influence in the Counties Council in the interest of the school. He was chairman during 1862-64; and, on his retiring at the end of '64, was warmly thanked by the other members for his efficient services.

Alexander McDonell was a wealthy farmer, who lived on the front about midway between Iroquois and Morrisburg, a son-in-law of Mr. Jacob Brouse, and a most decided Conservative in politics: he was very much in touch with the majority of the people in the Township, was Reeve in 1855, again in 1860 and 1861, and the third time in 1867, 1868 and 1869; he was never defeated, and appeared to have merely to ask from the people to receive. He became a Trustee in 1860, but never took very much interest in the school, and was not among its friends in the Council, at least not to the extent of granting much financial aid.

Dr. Addison Worthington was born in the County of Prescott, of American parents, was a millwright when he came to Matilda, and married the daughter of Mr. Peter Carman. He subsequently studied medicine under Dr. Alex. Wylie, and commenced practice here in 1851. In 1861 he was appointed Trustee, but moved to Howick in the following year.

Dr. J. D. R. Williams, his partner in business, was the eldest son of the Methodist missionary, W. H. Williams, spoken of in the early part of this work. Born in 1831, he graduated from the "Rolph School," Toronto, soon after Dr. Worthington began practice here, and became his partner. He was Reeve of the village in 1861; and in 1863 succeeded Dr. Worthington as Trustee. He left a few years later, has since been a newspaper writer, a mining speculator, and is now practising medicine in the neighboring village of Cardinal.

The principal difficulty with which the Trustees had to contend at this time was the financial one. They had the Government grant and the fees, which, under favorable conditions, were about sufficient to pay salaries; but any failure on the part of the teacher to secure or retain the approval of the patrons, led to the withdrawal of the pupils, and was almost certain to involve the Board in debt, and render their task of providing the ways and means, and of maintaining a proper equipment anything but a sinecure.

The law provided that the County Council might grant such aid as was needed, but these grants were voluntary, and the Councillors, elected by constituents, few of whom felt that they had any interest in higher education, were slow to respond to the appeal of the Trustees. The feeling that was some years later voiced by a member from the Township of Oznabruck, when he said that he did not "think it was fair for the poor people of Finch and Roxborough to be compelled to draw hoppoles twenty miles in order to educate the gentlemen's sons of Cornwall," no doubt existed to some extent throughout all the townships at the time of which we are writing. Besides, the sixth decade of this century was pre-eminently the age of *laissez faire;* the economic doctrines of Adam Smith and the Mills were all but universally accepted throughout the British Empire. In Great Britain the State had ceased to interfere with the course of trade ; in Canada we had, or thought we had, got rid of all State interference with the religion of the people. A new era appeared to be dawning; it was then held by advanced thinkers that the duty of the State was done when it had made and administered laws for the security of the life, the liberty and the property of the individual. It was the age when individualism and unrestricted competition were regarded by most thinking men as the proper and only reasonable rule of life. The gospel of Herbert Spencer, which teaches that the State is an organism with innumerable functions that it properly and necessarily exercises in the interest of the whole, had not yet been preached. We had in our progress toward a higher or more complex social life, reached the age when the right of one individual to dominate the life or conduct of another was no longer recognized ; we were only at the portals of the period when each unit of the social organism is made to feel its obligation to the whole, and is required to perform its part in promoting the general welfare.

It is true that Dr. Ryerson had been touring the country in behalf of free, common, or public schools, and had made some progress towards the desired end ; but few then thought of applying the principle of general taxation for the support of a system of education in which the mass of the people had, or felt they had, no share.

We have no record from which we can ascertain what were the revenues of the school during Mr. Carman's incumbency, further than that he received $600 per year, and his assistant $300. From this it would appear that it must have been nearly $1000 ; $400 of this was derived from the Government grant, a little, perhaps fifty, from rent of the living rooms in which a boarding-house was kept; leaving about $550 from fees. The fees were two, three, and four dollars for common English, higher English and classics, respectively, per term—four terms in the year. There would also be a little for music and drawing, which were taught by the assistant.

SEMI-CENTENNIAL OF IROQUOIS HIGH SCHOOL. 53

As the yearly average for each pupil—assuming half of them to be in the common branches only—would be a little over ten dollars, the average attendance must have been about fifty. At that time, however, there was no entrance examination to face, and a goodly number of young people took advantage of the winter terms; so the attendance was larger during that period, and correspondingly less in summer.

Very soon after Mr. Davies came the falling off in attendance must have been considerable, for before the year 1857 closed the services of the assistant had been dispensed with, and the total income of the school in 1858 was but $548.75. Nor does this indicate the full decline of the school under Mr. Davies, for one item of this was a Government grant of $200.00 for the last half of 1857, while the Goverment grant for the first half of 1858 was but $112.00; the remaining $231.75 was nearly all from fees. The next year Mr. Cowan made a much better showing, though the Government grant, based on the work done in the last half of 1858, was very small. The receipts were:

Tuition fees, first quarter............	$98 25	
Tuition fees, second quarter	92 00	
Tuition fees, third quarter	73 00	
Tuition fees, fourth quarter..........	65 25	
		$328 50
Government grant, first half-year	$94 00	
Government grant, second half-year ..	198 00	
		$292 00
Rent from room...........................		9 00
Total.............................		$629 50

The receipts in 1860 were:

Tuition fees, first quarter............	$69 00	
Tuition fees, second quarter	51 00	
Tuition fees, third quarter	61 25	
Tuition fees, fourth quarter..........	40 50	
		$221 75
Government grant, first half-year	$198 00	
Government grant, second half-year ..	190 00	
		$388 00
From Counties Council		150 00
Total.............................		$759 75

The first grant from the Counties Council was made in 1857. At the first meeting of the Trustees in that year a resolution was passed setting forth that the school grounds needed fencing and the building repairing; that maps, apparatus, etc., were required for the school; that the law provided that the Trustees might apply to the Counties Council for such sums as were necessary for the purposes specified, and directing the Chairman to ask the Counties Council at its next meeting to grant £50. This was responded to by a grant of £30. The members of the Counties Council from this County were: John Laing and George J. Brouse, Matilda; Henry H. Bolton, Mountain; James Holden and Henry Weegar, Williamsburg; Giles W. Bogart and James Irvine, Winchester.

The next grant asked for was in 1859. The institution was about $150 in debt, and a kitchen and woodshed were required. The amount asked for was $400, and the amount granted the $150 above, which was paid in the January following.

The members of Council from this County that year were: Philip Carman, Iroquois; George J. Brouse and Robert Toye, Matilda; George Mulloy and Mr. Farrel, Mountain; A. B. Sherman and Thomas Johnson, Williamsburg; G. W. Bogart and David Rae, Winchester.

The grant being insufficient, the new buildings were not proceeded with, but a new fence was built, and $50.00 was expended on maps, apparatus, etc. These included, we believe, an orrery, a very desirable piece of school furniture which the much more fully-equipped school of to-day does not possess. No further grant was made from the Counties until 1864, when $200.00 was given, supplemented the following January by $176.00 more, thus insuring the erection of the long-desired buildings.

The members from this county were, in 1864: Philip Carman, Iroquois; Robert Toye and Robert Lowery, Matilda; Henry Wallace and George Mulloy, Mountain; A. B. Sherman and John Sergeant, Williamsburg; David Rae and Orin C. Wood, Winchester; A. G. McDonell, Morrisburg.

In 1865 Matilda was represented by Robert Toye and Mr. Brouse; Mountain, by Thos. Bailey and Duncan Christie; Winchester, by O. C. Wood and Matthew Rae; the others remaining unchanged. In each of these lists the first named is the Reeve and the second the Deputy-Reeve. In 1857 Mountain had no Deputy-Reeve, and of course the villages had none.

We have given these gentlemen's names because every grant that was made to the school was used against them in the Townships, and sometimes to their undoing. Most of them deserved well of the friends of education.

The subsequent grants from the Counties Council were:

```
January, 1867 ........................... ...... $100
October,   "   ............................... 360
           1868 ............................... 100
           1869 ............................... 100
           1870 ............................... 100
```

All grants subsequent to 1866 were made for a *quid pro quo*. At the first meeting of the High School Board in that year, on the 7th February, it was

"Moved by Wm. Elliot, seconded by R. Toye, That in accordance with the condition of the report of the Committee on Schools from the United Counties of Stormont, Dundas and Glengarry, the Iroquois Grammar School be free from tuition fees to all pupils attending said school, and who reside more than two miles in any direction from the school, within the County, after the expiration of the present term." Carried.

In 1871 the law was changed, and thereafter the Counties Council was required to grant each year a sum equivalent to one-half of the Government grant.

The first assistance given by the village as a corporation was $60.00 in 1861. In 1864, $100.00 was given, and a like amount in each of the three years, 1868, 1869 and 1870.

CHAPTER VIII.

Mr. Whitney—Farming Out the School—Miss Bailey—Success—Government Grants—Local Apathy—The Morrisburg School—Changes in the Law—Formation of High School Districts—Model School—Abolition of the Districts.

N APRIL, 1860, Mr. Whitney took charge of the school to fill out Mr. Cowan's time. A mere temporary arrangement it seemed, and yet he had commenced what has been his life work. For over a quarter of a century he held the school—strong evidence in itself that he was well adapted for the profession he had chosen. He was born in the Township of Augusta, September 5th, 1834, had commenced teaching when but little over sixteen years of age, and from that time earned enough to enable him to, at intervals, prosecute his studies and go through college. He graduated in arts at Victoria just before he came here. A fellow student of Mr. Cowan, they were personal friends, and it was through that friendship he became the headmaster of the Iroquois Grammar School. On June 25th, 1860, he was engaged at $600 per year. That was the salary that had been paid for several years, and we have seen that the revenues of the school for some time had been barely sufficient to meet it without keeping an assistant. But Mr. Whitney, who was a shrewd business man as well as an efficient teacher, saw the possibilities of the institution's future if the stimulus of gain were added to the natural desire of the master to promote the interests of his school; and, after the end of his second term, proposed to take over the school

PHILO WHITNEY.
WM. A. WHITNEY, M.A.
CHARLES POTTER, B.A.
MRS. WM. L. REDMOND.
WM. MONTGOMERY, B.A.

and keep an assistant if the Government grant and fees were handed to him. This was accepted by the Trustees, and the new arrangement became operative at the middle of the fall term in 1860.

One of the first things Mr. Whitney did was to engage Miss Elizabeth Bailey as assistant, at $300 per year. Miss Bailey was a sister of Mrs. John A. Carman, and was known to be a good music teacher, and, we believe, was teaching a class in the village at the time.

The result fully justified Mr. Whitney's expectations. The first year, or, in 1861, the income from fees alone was $611; this, with a Government grant of $387, paid his assistant and left him a very comfortable increase of salary. We have no record of the following year, but about this time Miss Bailey retired from the school, and was married to Mr. William C. Bailey; thereafter music occupied a minor place on the curriculum, and the income from fees was much less. In 1863 it had fallen to $439, and the Government grant to $374; the assistant being paid but $150. The next year the figures were $452, $397 and $200, showing a gain all round, which was maintained until 1867, when the typhoid fever scourge temporarily checked the progress of the school.

As has been said, the care of our Government for education began at the top. Our universities were the first to receive attention; then the Grammar Schools, and lastly the Public Schools, on the principle, we suppose, that while growth is from the bottom upward, light and heat came down from above. At this time the Grammar Schools were regarded less as a training ground for teachers, or as places where the sons of merchants and farmers might get an education superior to that provided in the common schools, than as feeders for the universities. In pursuance of this idea, great importance was attached to the classics, and the size of the Government grant depended largely on the number of Latin students. For instance, in 1864, Iroquois had seventy-two English and twenty Latin pupils, and drew $397; while Williamstown, with thirty-seven English and thirty-two Latin pupils, received

$550. Other years about that time, and comparison with other schools, give similar results. The total attendance is not given in either case, but the English pupils probably included the whole school, though in some cases there may have been students who confined their studies entirely to the classics.

Mr. Whitney appears to have noted the circumstance, and to have governed himself accordingly; for, a few years later, the number of Latin pupils had increased to 86 per cent. of the total attendance, and the Legislative grant had more than doubled. In 1872 it was $993, and in 1873, $903.24; while the County, which, after 1871, was required to grant an amount equal to one-half of the Legislative grant, contributed, in the latter year, $528. The attendance was also good—112 pupils, ninety-seven of whom were in Latin, being given in the returns. Of the 109 High Schools then in the Province, only twenty, and these all in cities and towns, surpassed this school in this respect. It was the largest school east of Kingston, only two others, Brockville and Ottawa, having more than one hundred pupils. Mr. Whitney's salary was $800, and that of his brother, Philo, his assistant, $400.

In 1869 the Board had been enabled, by a grant from the Counties Council, to increase the school accommodation, by removing the sleeping apartments and throwing the whole upper flat into one large school-room; so to the people and the municipal authorities, and perhaps to Mr. Whitney also, nothing more seemed to be required. The first were getting a High-school education for their children without having to contribute thereto themselves, the second were relieved of the necessity of assisting a local public institution that had been provided for them free of cost, and was of great commercial, as well as educational advantage to the place, while the last was prospering on his moderate salary, and had no desire to disturb the existing conditions. Perhaps it would be unfair to say that they were being afflicted with the malady that Mr. Philip Carman had deplored in Mr. Dick twenty years before, but there is little doubt but the exceptionally favorable conditions under which this school was placed from 1869 to 1874 tended to produce an unwillingness on the part of the people and the Council of the village to bear a fair share of the cost of maintenance. This subsequently proved injurious, almost disastrous, to the institution; and when the evil days came Mr. Whitney was made the scapegoat, and had to suffer for sins not his own. If ever it is desirable to make hay when the sun shines, most assuredly the time to strengthen the teaching staff, improve the equipment, and, if necessary, enlarge the building, was when the whole cost of the school, even to making the fires and sweeping-out the rooms, was provided from outside. The aid given by the Government was intended to promote, not to destroy, local effort. It should have been obvious to the most obtuse, that the conditions then existing could not continue; besides, the Morrisburg people had, in 1865, established a Grammar School in connection with their Public School. That village was somewhat larger than this, was nearer the centre of the county, and, having the Registry Office, was, in a sense, the county town of the County of Dundas. Its rivalry had not yet proved formidable, but it could even then be seen that unless a little of the spirit of the men of 1845 remained with their successors, the Iroquois school would soon cease to be the chief seat of learning in the county.

The law as it affected Grammar Schools had remained without material alteration from 1854 to 1871. In the latter year the office of Chief Superintendent of Education was abolished, and the Department placed under the control of a member of the Government, called the Minister of Education. Several changes were made, one of the least of them being that Grammar Schools were thereafter to be called High Schools. The principal changes that affected schools outside of the cities were four in number: the first provided that the County Council, while still empowered to make voluntary grants, must grant a sum each year equal to at least one-half of the Legislative grant; the second authorized that body to form the whole or a part or parts of the county into a High School district or districts; the third directed that any further sums, beyond the Legislative and Municipal grants, and fees, required for the maintenance of the school, be paid, on the requisition of the High School Board, by the municipality in which the school is situated; or, in the event of a High School district or districts having been formed, by the municipalities, or parts of municipalities, forming such districts; and by the fourth—which held great, but alas! unrealized possibilities for Iroquois school—it was provided that any High School with four masters and not less than an average of sixty male pupils studying Latin or Greek, might become a Collegiate Institute, and as such receive an additional Legislative grant, not to exceed $750 per annum.

In 1874 some further changes were made; one new provision being that the High School grants be apportioned according to the average attendance of pupils and their proficiency in the various branches of study prescribed for High Schools and Collegiate Institutes, as ascertained by the High School Inspectors. Another required that all moneys apportioned by the Government, together with a sum provided by local municipal assessment, equal to half the amount, be applied in payment of salaries to masters and teachers. In 1877 the Municipal grant was made equal to the Legislative grant, and both were still to be applied in payment of teachers.

The Act of 1874 changed the source from which the Trustees received their appointment. Hitherto they had all been appointed by the counties, but now that they were authorized to call on the municipality in which the school was situated, to make good any deficiency left after the Legislative and County grants had been used, it was provided that three of them be appointed by the County Council and three by the Council of the municipality in which the school was situated. The Acts of 1871 and 1874 gave County Councils the power to form districts and define their limits; but this power was withdrawn in 1877, though they were still left the power to abolish. A want of a clear understanding of this last change caused considerable litigation and involved these counties in a heavy bill of costs, when the districts in which this county was divided were abolished in 1878.

In 1885 the mode of apportionment of the Legislative grant was again changed, and based on the salaries paid to masters and assistants, the character and equipment of the school buildings and appendages, and on the average attendance of pupils. These changes appear to have been designed to increase the general efficiency of the High Schools by giving them an assured income, and by adapting them more and more to the municipal institutions of the country, as well as by increasing the Government supervision and control. They tended also to relatively reduce the contributions from the Government, and to increase those from the County and Local Councils. This was inevitable if the schools were to become an integral part of the educational system of the country, and was not in itself undesirable, but in the transition there was a good deal of friction. There was not only the very natural desire among the people to avoid new inposts; but until the Municipal Amendment Act of 1889, excluding members of Municipal Councils, was passed, the rule was for Reeves to accept appointments as Trustees of High Schools. Their first care very frequently was for their municipal positions, on which the others sometimes depended, and for the retention of which no plea was deemed so effective as that they had kept down the taxes.

This appears to have been the guiding principle that in High School matters actuated the municipal authorities of Iroquois for some years after the change in the law made in 1871. They took no heed of the admonition: "There is that scattereth, and yet increaseth; and there is that withholdeth more than is meet, but it tendeth to poverty."

At the first session of the Counties Council, after the passing of the Act of 1871, a by-law was passed, forming this county into High School districts; Matilda and Mountain being given to Iroquois, while the eastern part of the county was given to Morrisburg. Had this been done with a full knowledge on the part of the Reeves from the townships of the position in which their municipalities were being placed in relation to the High School Board, it would have been of great advantage to the village and to the school; that is, had the townships voluntarily agreed to pay *pro rata* with the people of Iroquois the whole cost of equipping and maintaining the High School. But the law was a new one, the statutes had not yet been generally distributed: few members of the Council had seen them; and fewer still knew the real purport of the recent enactments. The impression was created that it was as necessary to divide the whole County into High School districts as it was to divide the whole Township into Public School sections, and in this way the measure was carried. Of course, the village representatives had the statutes, and it is probable they had studied them sufficiently to know that what was proposed would be of advantage to their constituents, but they do not appear to have got much farther, for we find them the same session levying the County grant on the district, instead of on the county, thereby taking from this district, which had the largest school, very much more in proportion to the assessment than was exacted from any other part of the counties.

The by-law, however, did not for some time affect the school or the rates. The County and Legislative grants were amply sufficient for the school as then conducted, and in the following year the fees were removed, and the school became free. It was not until 1876, when its prosperity began to wane, and the apportionment under the Act of 1874, which proved less favorable than that under previous Acts, began to be felt, that it became necessary to call on the district.

The calls were at first light, $300 in 1876 and $423 in 1877, and were little felt; and, notwithstanding one-half of the Trustees were chosen by the village Council, thus making the arrangement seem more unfair, the districts might have been continued had it not been for the action of the Morrisburg School Board. The Morrisburg School was a Union, Public and High School, with twelve Trustees, nine of whom were chosen by the people and Council of the village and three by the Counties Council. It had up to this time been kept in the Public school buildings. The Morrisburg people had not only been less modest in their demands, but they had resolved to build a new High School, and levy the cost on their district.

They had just got the model school there. Mr. Brown was appointed inspector, and his office would be there, and the time was opportune to push the Morrisburg High School to the front.

In the January Session, 1878, M. F. Beach, who was then Deputy-Reeve of Winchester, introduced a by-law to relieve the Township, but failed to carry it; and as the eastern members were largely in sympathy with the representatives from the villages, it might not have been possible to carry it at any time had it not been for another feature in the law relating to High Schools. By the Municipal Act a union of counties was regarded as a single county, except for registration purposes. But while the grants were voluntary, it had been customary for each county to contribute to the school or schools within its borders. When they became obligatory, and the Dundas schools being the largest, became entitled to nearly one-half the money required to meet the Government grants within the counties, the members from this county contended for a *pro rata* assessment over the three counties, while their eastern confreres insisted on continuing the old system, whereby each County provided for its own schools; and as they possessed the necessary voting power, they were enabled to enforce their views, unless their western friends should resort to the courts of law for redress. This was frequently threatened, but not proceeded with until 1877, when Dr. Chamberlain, Reeve of Morrisburg, made application to have the by-law of that year quashed, on the ground that the levy was not uniform over the whole of the united counties, and was, of course, successful. The eastern men then, through their representatives in the Local Legislature, got the law changed so that any one County, through its Reeves, might, for High School purposes, withdraw from a union of counties. Acting on this, in the June session of 1878, Glengarry and Stormont both withdrew, so that each of the three counties became a separate county for High School purposes. And now that the smaller villages were deprived of their eastern support, Mr. Beach had no further difficulty in getting a by-law through the Council abolishing the High School districts in this County. This by-law was also attacked in the courts on a technicality, and for a time successfully, but the clause abolishing the High School districts was finally sustained.

SOLOMON DORAN.   CEPHAS MILLS.
ROBERT TOYE.   JOHN N. TUTTLE.

CHAPTER IX.

Mr. Whitney (*continued*)—Revenues and Salaries—Assistants—New Trustees—Edward Parlow—Robert Toye—Solomon Doran—James Stephenson, M.D.—John N. Tuttle—John Harkness, M.D.—Geo. Steacy, M.D.—James A. Carman, B.A.—Declining Prosperity—The New Woman—Public Buildings—School Neglected.

ROM the time the school was farmed out to Mr. Whitney in 1861 until 1870 there is no complete record of income or expenditure, the Trustees having no finances to deal with but those affecting repairs, improvements or equipment. As changes in the law and regulations were very frequent during the next decade, we give a statement of the revenues of the school, showing the sources from which they were derived. The figures illustrate one phase of the progress of the High School from the State aid and local control that marked the earlier period of its history towards the State control and local taxation that followed the establishment of a Department of Education with a member of the Government, as Minister, at its head.

Year.	Legislative Grant.	County Grant.	Village Grant.	High School District.	Fees.	Readings, Etc.	Total Revenue.
1870	$734 00	$100 00	$100 00	....	$204 76	$76 19	$1215 35
1871	914 00	360 00	....	....	151 19	....	1425 19
1872	993 00	479 50	....	....	33 10	....	1505 60
1873	903 24	503 90	....	....	....	....	1407 14
1874	864 00	470 00	....	....	....	....	1334 00
1875	802 60	400 00	....	....	13 00	....	1215 60
1876	567 50	500 00	....	$300 00	114 50	....	1482 00
1877	523 50	500 00	50 00	400 00	81 00	....	1554 50
1878	536 08	525 00	40 00	*240 73	73 00	....	1414 81
1879	532 50	590 00	....	....	105 00	....	1227 50
1880	584 99	650 .)	200 00	....	90 00	....	1524 99

*This and the $40 from Iroquois were part of a levy of $450 made on the District after it had been abolished, and which the Mountain Council refused to recognize.

We are almost equally in the dark with reference to the assistants. The falling off in receipts from fees after 1861 would seem to indicate that Miss Bailey, from whose music lessons a considerable proportion of these was derived, was no longer in the school. In the early part of 1861, Mr. Whitney married one of his pupils, Miss Mary Rose, a niece of the Charles C. Rose who, with others, tried to establish a Grammar School in 1843. This lady was assistant for a time, as were also a Miss Weagant, of Morrisburg: Miss Stephens; Miss Holden, a daughter of James Holden, of Morrisburg: Mr. H. H. Ross, and a Mr. Service. How long any of these taught or in what order they came and went, or what remuneration they received we have no means of knowing, as it is not till 1869, or after the school was again taken over by the Trustees, that we have any record.

In that year Miss Annie Carman, youngest daughter of Mr. Philip Carman, a young lady who had just taken the degree of "Mistress of English Literature" from Albert College, was engaged as assistant. The salary does not appear to have been fixed at the time, but she received for work in that year $195, and a Miss Shaver received $15. It is probable that between them they did not put in a full year. From that on we can give the names of the assistants and the salaries paid:

Year.	Name.	Assistants' Salaries.	Master's Salary.
1868..		....	$650 00
1869..	Annie Carman	$275 00	700 00
1870..	" "	275 00	700 00
1871..	Miss Lane	250 00	700 00
1872..	{ John Reid Ross { James A. Carman	122 80 } 105 00 }	750 00
1873..	Philo Whitney	400 00	800 00
1874..	" "	475 00	850 00
1875..	" "	500 00	900 00
1876..	{ J. S. Clough { H. T. Leslie	225 00 } 200 00 }	900 00
1877..	{ H. T. Leslie { John A. D. Hamilton	400 00 }	800 00
1878..	W. F. W. Creelman	400 00	800 00
1879..	A. C. Crosby	400 00	800 00
1880..	Alex. McLeod	400 00	800 00

Comparing these figures with the revenue for the same period, we find that the total grants from the Government and counties for the first five years were, in round figures, $6,700, while the salaries paid teachers were but $5,850, and the contribution from local sources less than $200. Though it was not definitely so expressed in the statutes, these grants were intended, by the Department of Education, to be applied in payment of teachers' salaries, and we find it in 1875 making representations to the High School Board to the effect that they had been misapplied. The Board at once, on motion of Dr. Harkness, seconded by Robert Toye, resolved, "That all moneys hereafter received be applied strictly as the law directs." The wording of the statute was soon after amended so as to leave no room for difference of opinion as to the disposition to be made of these grants.

If we except Miss Carman, who taught two years, and Mr. Philo Whitney, who remained in the school a little over three, none of the assistants appear to have remained more than a year, and several of them only a few months. They were mostly students out of a job, and the Iroquois High School appears to have added one more to its many claims on the gratitude of the public, by thus helping them on their way up the hill of knowledge.

After the opening of the Grammar School in Morrisburg the representatives from the eastern part of the County retired from the Board, and the names we meet in the minutes between that and 1880, are the three old members, Messrs. Carman, Elliot and Ross, the first retiring in 1875, the second in 1878, and the last in 1879; Dr. Williams, who was in at the time, but whose name does not appear after 1866, and Edward Parlow, Dr. Samuel Cowan, Robert Toye, Solomon Doran, Dr. James Stephenson, John N. Tuttle, Dr. John Harkness, Dr. George Steacy and James A. Carman, new men, who came in from time to time during the interval.

Edward Parlow, B.A., was first appointed in 1866, and served nine years. He was the son of John Parlow, Esq., a wealthy farmer, who lived three miles east of the village, was young, unmarried, and well educated. He attended the meetings of the Board regularly, but rarely took a leading part, or attempted to exert much influence on the Board or the school.

Mr. Cowan's career has already been noticed.

Robert Toye was born in Ireland in 1821, and came to Canada when a very young man. He taught school a short time, but married early and settled on a farm in the Eighth Concession of Matilda, then the "Haggerty settlement," now Toye's Hill. His superior education and ability soon made him a local leader. In 1857 he was first elected a member of the Matilda Council; in 1859 he became Deputy-Reeve, and in 1862, Reeve. This position he held for five years, and took a prominent part in the business of the Counties Council. Whether from early association, or a true appreciation of its worth, or from both combined, he was always a friend of education, and supported the school in the Counties Council at some risk to his popularity in the township. In 1866 he became a Trustee, and from that time until 1879, when he succeeded Mr. Ross as chairman, he was an efficient and indefatigable worker in behalf of the school. The story of his withdrawal may bear repeating, and may convey its lesson. Soon after he ceased to be a member of the Matilda Council he was appointed Lockmaster at the head of the Williamsburg Canal. This place is a little nearer Morrisburg than Iroquois, but that made no difference in his attitude toward the respective schools. In 1879 he was again elected Reeve of the township. He never stood so high in the esteem of the people as he did at that time, but he succeeded a western man who opposed him relentlessly. Complaint was made that he held a municipal office, contrary to the regulations governing the Civil Service. The complaint was drawn up by the Secretary of the School Board, Mr. Tuttle. Some other members of the Board were suspected of being parties to it, and the sympathies of the people of Iroquois were, or seemed to be, against him. He resigned the Reeveship, and at the end of the year withdrew from the Board and the school.

Mr. Solomon Doran was the son of Edmund Doran, an American, who had come to Canada early in the century, and settled a mile and a half east of Iroquois. The old gentleman's father was a Vermont Irishman, and his mother a Beecher; and with the industry and capacity for hard work characteristic of his father's countrymen, combined with the shrewdness of the Yankee, he had succeeded in amassing considerable wealth. His youngest son, the subject of this sketch, devoted his attention partly to farming, but principally to dealing in grain and speculating. During the sixties he built a large block in the village, and formed a partnership with Richard Oxnam, a miller, William Bailey, a merchant, and Laughlin Cameron, a millowner: purchased Elliot's and Cameron's mills, and for some years conducted a large mercantile and milling business. He was also a member of the village Council and Chairman of the Methodist Church Building Committee. In 1875 he was appointed a member of the High School Board, and died soon after. What he might have done for the school was left for his son, who succeeded him in business, and who did it very well ten years later.

Dr. James Stephenson succeeded him. The Doctor was a native of the County of Grenville, and a graduate of McGill College. He had commenced the practice of medicine here about the same time that Mr. Whitney began in the school. They were of the same age, both having been born in September, 1834. The Doctor won popular favor very rapidly, and soon had a large practice. In 1869 he succeeded Mr. Philip Carman as Reeve of the village, and held the position without question until the close of 1875, when he voluntarily retired. At the time his influence was confessedly greater than that of any other man in the place, but he appears to have taken but a languid interest in school matters, and abandoned the Trusteeship at the end of his term, in 1877.

John N. Tuttle, who had served a long time as village Clerk and Councillor, was elected Reeve in 1876, and appointed a member of the High School Board by the village

Council in place of Mr. Philip Carman, whom he also succeeded as Secretary-Treasurer. Mr. Tuttle first saw the light at what is now Dundela, in the Township of Matilda, in September, 1834, the natal year and month of Mr. Whitney and Dr. Stephenson. His father, Elijah, was descended from one of the "old families," and was a farmer and local Methodist preacher and exhorter. When a boy young Tuttle entered the store of Messrs. Jacob Brouse and Wm. Bailey as clerk. Some years later he started a mercantile business on his own account, but after a few years abandoned that and became a conveyancer and insurance agent. He was a shrewd business man, a keen politician, an active worker in the interests of the Liberal party, and for several years an influential member of the High School Board; was Secretary-Treasurer until 1888, when failing health compelled him to resign, and at the close of that year he retired from the Trusteeship. Except one year he was Reeve of the village from 1876 to the close of 1882, in which year he was appointed to the office of Division Court Clerk, which he still holds.

Outside of the village of Iroquois no man has taken so lively an interest in the fortunes of the High School, or done so much to promote its welfare, as Dr. John Harkness. His father, John Harkness, was a North of Ireland Presbyterian, who came to Canada in 1820; his mother, the daughter of a U.E. Loyalist. They settled in the Third Concession of Matilda in 1826, where their fourth son, John, was born on the 10th of May, 1841. He entered the Matilda Grammar School in 1854; beginning when Mr. Albert Carman became the master, he remained a pupil until 1857—both he and the master quitting the school at the same time. He must have been an exceptionally good student, for when barely fifteen years of age he went before the County examiners and took a first-class teacher's certificate. He graduated in medicine at McGill in 1862, and soon after settled on the Homestead, where he has since lived, devoting his attention principally to his practice, his farm, and his library, which latter is well-stocked with scientific and philosophic works. A close student and deep thinker, he has kept *en rapport* with the ablest scientific writers of his time, Darwin, Huxley, Tyndall and Spencer being among his favorites. A Conservative in politics, he has never been an active politician, the time that he has had to spare for public affairs having been almost entirely devoted to the interests of education. He was Superintendent of Schools for the Township of Matilda for the three years ending in 1866: has been Trustee of the Public School at Irena, near his home, about thirty years; and it is one of the best country schools to be found anywhere. In 1875 he was first appointed Trustee of Iroquois High School, but was dropped the next year, it was said, because he favored increased expenditure and efficiency. He was, however, reappointed in 1878, and in 1880 became Chairman of the Board, and has filled that position every year since save one.

Dr. George Steacy was a physician in good practice at South Mountain. He was first appointed in 1876. He remained a member six years; was a man of ability, but resided at such a distance that he was unable to attend the meetings regularly.

James A. Carman was the eldest son of John A. Carman, the founder of the school. Born in 1851, he was among Mr. Whitney's pupils in the High School. In 1872 he graduated in arts at Albert College, and in 1877 commenced business in Iroquois as a partner of his father. In 1879 he was appointed to the High School Board. He does not appear to have, at that time, even contemplated adopting teaching as a profession, and the special gifts that enabled him a few years later, as Principal, to raise the Iroquois School to a higher plane were yet in the womb of the future.

During the later years of the seventies the prosperity of the school appears to have been declining, and the attendance had fallen from an aggregate of 112, in 1873, to about 75, with an average of not more than fifty, the two or three last years of the decade. This was partly due to causes already indicated, and to the imposition of fees and restrictions on the entrance of new pupils. It was probably due also, to some extent, to causes operative on a much wider field. The general prosperity so characteristic of the fifties was, with some intervals of depression, maintained through and beyond the next decade. The wars that began with the American war of secession in 1861, and terminated with the Franco-German war in 1870, had stimulated prices in all countries, while the extensive public works undertaken in Canada, immediately after and consequent on the Confederation of the Provinces in 1867 made the outlook very hopeful here for several years. About 1874 a reaction set in, due largely to the demonetization of silver in the principal European countries, and in the United States. The conditions of the sixth decade were reversed in the eighth. The demand for gold to replace the silver was enormous, its price went up, and that of every other commodity, of which it was the measure, went down accordingly. Canada was not only a borrowing country, but her fiscal system was so arranged that she felt the full force of the current of depression. One of the most important industries in this village collapsed altogether, every business languished, the wheels of progress, if not actually turned back, were stayed.

In this age of the "New Woman," when the "ladies" are coming to the front so rapidly in our schools and colleges, when two-thirds of the teachers in our Public Schools, and a considerable proportion of those in our High Schools and Collegiate Institutes are women, it seems passing strange that the Government was so slow to recognize the value, to that very necessary part of the social organism, of higher education. We have already seen that in the earlier years of the Grammar School nearly the whole of the grant was given to encourage the study of Latin and Greek, subjects not usually taken up by girls; and so late as 1868, it was seriously proposed to exclude women from the Grammar Schools, or if not to absolutely exclude them, to at least refuse to count them in apportioning the grants. As in 1852, when pleading for local control, our Trustees appeared to be in advance of the authorities at the seat of Government.

The matter was taken up at a meeting held in July of that year (1868), the members present being: J. S. Ross, Chairman; Philip Carman, Secretary, and Messrs. William Elliot, Robert Toye and Edward Parlow.

After, on motion of Mr. Carman, seconded by Mr. Parlow, expressing concurrence in the views expressed in a circular from the Colborne Grammar School, respecting the distribution of the Government grant to Grammar Schools, it was, on motion of Mr. Toye, seconded by Mr. Elliot,

Resolved,—" That in the opinion of the Board, the privilege heretofore extended to girls in admitting them as Grammar School pupils, is recognized as one of the greatest advantages of our educational institutions, and that any scheme adopted by the Chief Superintendent to prohibit them from participating in the advantages of a more liberal and superior education than can be obtained in a common school would have a most baneful and prejudicial effect on the community, and this Board is prepared to give their assistance in promoting such measures as will maintain the Grammar Schools in their former standing in accordance with the Grammar School law."

The sinister intention of the Chief Superintendent never became law, but the School Act of 1871 gave no credit for any but male pupils in establishing Collegiate Institutes, and it was not until 1874 that the sexes were placed on an equality in reference to the Government grants.

Very early in the century there was a Methodist Church built on the " Point," about half a mile west of the future site of the village, and a sort of joint Anglican and Presbyterian Church on the commons, a mile east. The Methodist Church was subsequently replaced by a substantial stone structure on the site of the present cemetery, and about 1834 the other church fell entirely into the hands of the Church of England people. These two were the only churches in the front of Matilda, or in the Township, when this village began to take form. The church on the "Point" had become a Wesleyan Church, and, in 1855, that body built a new church in the heart of the village, on the site of the present one, given by Mr. George Brouse. Some years later, in 1864, the Church of England people erected their beautiful little Gothic edifice on the site of a flax mill that had been built during the cotton famine, incident to the American Civil War, and burned soon after.

About the same time the Methodist Episcopal Church near the west end of College Street—now the Catholic Church—was erected.

The Presbyterians were few in number, but zealous, and mainly by the efforts of Mr. Elliot, who contributed the site and otherwise helped the enterprise liberally, their little brick church, on the corner of College and Harriet Streets, was completed in 1874. 1876 witnessed the supreme effort in church building, when the Wesleyan Methodists replaced their old building, which had been faultily constructed, by the present fine structure, costing about $15,000.

The little school-house to which we were introduced at the beginning of this work, soon proved too small for the increasing number of children, and a new school-house, slightly larger on the ground, and two stories in height, was built on College Street. The old building, that was to have been the nucleus of a Grammar School, was then used first as a dwelling and confectioner's shop, then as a harness shop, and finally as a butcher shop. It was a little like taking the "dust of Cæsar to stuff a cranny," but all the while it served a useful purpose, until removed in 1892, by Mr. William Fisher, to make room for his present shop. The College Street building was soon filled to overflowing, and, in 1876, the present Public school building was erected. It accommodates five teachers and from two to three hundred pupils, but it needs enlarging.

In 1875 the Town Hall, two stories and 40 x 70 feet, was erected at a cost of about $6,000.

In the thirteen years from 1864 to 1876 about $40,000 had been spent in public buildings. The Public school was fairly abreast of the time. The Town Hall was an exceptionally good one for a village of one thousand inhabitants. The

VIEW OF VILLAGE.

churches were beyond the needs of the people, and provided with every necessary accessory to make the act of worship easy and agreeable.

The one institution that was neglected during all this time, and for ten years afterward, was the High School. To the onlooker this seemed strange, as, putting it on the lowest ground, it had a money value to the people greater, perhaps, than that of all the others combined. It provided an education at a nominal cost that practically was a life provision for the recipient. The result has proved that it was better to be the son of a poor man in or near the village with three or four years at the High School as a setting-out, than to come into a one or two thousand-dollar farm in the country with no such advantages. It also tended to draw people from considerable distances in the country, and extended the influence of the village far beyond its otherwise narrow circle. Besides, every dollar expended on it was sure to bring additional aid from the Government. But, perhaps, just here was the weak point. The churches, which were built by purely voluntary offerings, surpassed all the other buildings. The Town Hall, which was built by assessment, but entirely out of local funds, came next, followed by the public school, which received some Government aid. It may be that the paralyzing influence that is sometimes attributed to State churchism, extends to all other departments of life, and that we cannot have state-aided education without destroying or lessening the springs of private enterprise and individual effort.

CHAPTER X.

Mr. Whitney (*continued*)—Want of Equipment—New Assistants—Wm. Montgomery—Charles Potter—Inspectors' Reports—Business Outlook Improving—Added Trustees—Cephas and Mason Mills—Beginning of Trouble—Close of Whitney Regime.

ABOUT 1880, the school had settled down to a position that it maintained with difficulty for the four or five subsequent years. Morrisburg had the Model School, the Inspector of Public Schools, a fine new High School building, that was about to become the home of a Collegiate Institute, so the faces of the people seeking a superior education were turned in that direction. Mr. Whitney had earned a high reputation as a teacher, but that was practically all on which this school had to rely. Its equipment was inferior. Some of the assistants may have been, no doubt were, very good men, but their connection with the institution was, in each case, so brief, that there was no time to build any reputation, outside of that of headmaster, that would add additional strength; in fact, the salaries that had been and were being paid were so low that good men could not be retained. We have seen that in the ten years beginning in 1871 and ending in 1880, there had been eleven assistants, and in 1881 there was another, Mr. John M. Kinney, who remained but a year. Rather better success attended the next effort, when William Montgomery was engaged, at the beginning of 1882. Mr. Montgomery was born in Ireland, in 1859, but came to Canada when very young. In 1879 he matriculated from the Port Hope High School, and when he came here had been two years at

Toronto University, taking an honor course in mathematics and physics. He taught here two years and a half, giving evidence of the qualities that ensure success, but left in July, 1884, to finish his course at the University. He was succeeded by Charles Potter, B.A., a graduate of Toronto University. Mr. Potter, the son of a Methodist clergyman of literary tastes, was himself a man of more than average ability and attainments, and had had six years' experience as teacher. He and Whitney made the strongest staff the school had seen, and there is no doubt but good work was done at that time, but they were heavily handicapped by want of equipment and attendance. J. E. Hodgson visited the school in June, 1883, and reports the total number of pupils present thirty-eight, of whom fourteen boys and four girls were in Latin. He says, in his remarks, "This school is, in my opinion, well conducted and is doing good work."

In June, 1884, it was visited by High School Inspector J. A. McLellan. He found the total number of pupils fifty-eight, of whom forty-seven were present, nineteen being in Latin. He says: " I was very much pleased with the general intelligence of the class, and with their evident devotion to work."

The next visit was by Mr. Hodgson in September, 1885. He then found the total number enrolled fifty-eight, of whom thirty-nine were present. He is rather less commendatory this time, though he says, "Fair work is being done in this school, one pupil, preparing for senior matriculation, is very well up in his work."

The following year there was a new staff of teachers, and Mr. John Seath was Inspector. He evidently had taken to heart the admonition that it is not well to spare the rod and spoil the child, for he applies the lash unsparingly. We who have witnessed some of the results cannot but regret that it was not applied earlier. No one reading his report, and visiting the present school, can fail to be struck by the transformation that has taken place inside of ten years. He says nothing about the attendance or the efficiency of the teachers, but describes the premises, and as he found them:

Water supply: None.

School grounds: No ornamental trees; in very bad condition; no separate playgrounds; no separate entrances and walks; not well fenced.

School building: Very plain in appearance.

Class rooms: Inconveniently arranged; very dingy and ill-kept; walls papered, not tinted; floors in very bad condition; not separate entrances.

Lighting: Very bad; from all sides in the upper room, from three in lower room; windows small and placed low; not sufficient blinds.

Heating: One of the stoves in bad condition, and the other of poor appearance; no wood-box upstairs; only class rooms heated.

Ventilation: None of a satisfactory kind; windows not on pulleys; no fan-lights.

Halls: Not separate for the sexes, or with separate means of egress; no door-mats or scrapers; no porches. In very poor condition.

Waiting-rooms: None.

Cap rooms: One for the girls; in very poor condition.

Teachers' private rooms: None.

Desks: Double; poor in one room; no provision for teaching science.

Blackboards: Only boards of little value; badly situated with respect to the light.

EQUIPMENT AND REMARKS.

Library of reference: Number of items, five; value, $24.75. This should be increased to $250 at least.

Physical and chemical apparatus: A few bottles, worth probably $4. This also should be of the value of $250 at least.

Gymnasium: None.

Charts, maps and globes: Number of items, nine; value, $17.25. This part of the equipment is very poor. The latest maps, etc., should be provided.

GENERAL REMARKS.

As I pointed out to members of the Board, the only remedy for the existing defects is a careful renovation of the accommodations; this, I believe, the Board intends to make.

The equipment should be largely increased; as matters now stand it is not possible for the teachers to do good work.

The grading will not be made until the Board has sent me its report of the alterations proposed to be made before next July.

The late W. T. Benson, of Cardinal, while a member of the House of Commons, speaking of the Hon. Alex. McKenzie, said, that he owed his success in public life largely to his ability to find fault; he could do it easily, gracefully, and with an air of candor and complete conviction that was very effective. Mr. Seath is evidently slightly touched with the fire of the Hon. Alexander's genius; still, the picture, though a little highly colored, is not much overdrawn. The institution had been neglected, starved; it was shabby and out at elbows, and appeared to disadvantage among neighboring schools; it had become a purely local affair, and the question of wiping it out altogether was being seriously discussed by some of the Township representatives in the Counties Council. It had become obvious if Iroquois was to have a school at all worthy its traditions, that something effective must be done, and that speedily. Fortunately the times were propitious, and the men were not wanting.

The revival of business that was generally felt throughout the country about 1880, did not touch Iroquois until a little later. Early in 1883 the old flouring mill, built by Mr. Elliot more than thirty years before, was burned. It, like the school, had become "out of date," and its removal left vacant one of the best milling sites in the country. T. S. Edwards, a native of the Township of Oxford, who had previously acquired considerable wealth in the grocery trade in New York city, settled in Iroquois in 1879, and in 1883 succeeded Mr. Tuttle as Reeve. He at once interested himself in the matter, and by setting forth the advantages of the situation, and promising exemption from taxation for ten years, induced Mahlon F. Beach, a successful manufacturer, then located in Winchester, to build a large roller mill here. A little before this the stave business that had collapsed about 1875 was revived, by Arthur Patton. During the next year, 1884, Mr. Edwards introduced a by-law to provide for the construction of water works. This was defeated when submitted to the people, but the following year his successor, William M. Doran, successfully carried through a scheme whereby the water works were put in by a Company. When put in in this way the direct fiat of the people was not necessary, so they benefited in their own despite, though it is now, we believe, generally admitted that it had been better had they consented to become the owners of their own water supply. New and better buildings were going up here and there and everything about the place betokened improvement. The people were more hopeful, and the special merit of the men who had to do with High School affairs at this time is that they took advantage of the conditions prevailing to lift their institution to a much higher plane, and place it on the road to further progress and improvement.

The Trustees in 1880 were Dr. Harkness, Dr. Steacy and Samuel Robertson, appointees of the Counties Council, and Cephas Mills, John N. Tuttle and P. L. Palmer, representing the Village Council. I regard this year as the beginning of a sort of new period, not because there was anything important done at this time, or for three or four years thereafter, but because it is the first year in which Mr. Mills' name appears as a trustee, and because he and Dr. Harkness then became the most prominent members of the Board, first as chiefs of rival factions, contending over the principalship, and when that was settled, as leaders of a united body energetically engaged in carrying out improvements that have made the school one of the best in the country.

Mr. Mills was descended from an old Puritan family. His father Cephas Mills, was a Montreal merchant, whose business led him frequently to other cities. He was in New York in 1831, where his son Cephas was born. The young Cephas— the sixth or seventh of that name in the direct line—was educated at a private school and the High School, Montreal. When sixteen years of age he entered the store of the late Hon. John Young, then a grocer and provision merchant. He early interested himself in politics, for his name appears on the famous annexation manifesto of 1849, signed by so many young men who afterwards became prominent figures in the political life of the country.

In 1851 his mother, who had become a widow, was married to Jacob Brouse, Esq., of Matilda. This brought young Mills to Iroquois occasionally. He became interested in Mr. Brouse's youngest daughter, Nancy, and in 1858, the young people were married, Mr. Mills taking his father-in-law's place as partner with W. C. Bailey in a mercantile business in Iroquois. Soon after he started on his own account, and in 1861 was joined by his brother, Mason. Mason was born in 1836, in the City of Matanzas, on the Island of Cuba, whither his mother had gone for her health.

Both brothers had strong personalities. The elder, being the most studious, managed the books and the financial part of the business, while the younger and more active devoted himself to the selling department. The business extended rapidly, and has for over thirty years been the largest general store in the county.

No Damon and Pythias were ever more devoted to each other than these brothers. They were inseparable in business and in pleasure. When you saw one, you might be almost certain the other was near. In 1876 they went to the Centennial at Philadelphia together, and in 1881 made the "grand tour" in Europe. In 1887, while returning from a trip to Philadelphia on the ill-fated train that went down with the bridge at White River Junction, Vermont, "the one was taken and the other left." When approaching the bridge, Mason had gone forward to the smoking car, which reached the opposite bank of the river just as the structure gave way, precipitating the passenger cars to the bed of the stream thirty feet below.

Samuel Robertson was a farmer, living about three miles east of the village, who had been Deputy-Reeve of the Township in 1866. He remained on the Board until his death in 1885, but never took a very active interest in the affairs of the school.

P. L. Palmer was a practising barrister, who came to Iroquois about this time. He remained on the Board but a couple of years, when he removed to Denver on account of failing health. He is now one of the District Judges in that city.

There was no change made in the *personnel* of the Board in 1881, but the following year Dr. Colquhoun replaced Palmer, and A. B. Carman was appointed by the Counties Council in place of Dr. Steacy. Dr. Colquhoun was a graduate of McGill College, who settled here in 1879. He took an active interest in everything that tended to the educational advancement of the place, but was retained on the Board only three years.

A. B. Carman was the second son of John A. Carman, the founder of the school. He was an active member of the Board from the first. Succeeded Mr. Tuttle as Secretary and Treasurer in 1888, and continued to fill that office until, for reasons that will appear hereafter, he severed his connection with the Board in 1892.

About, or a little before 1883, Mr. Whitney began to have the experience of nearly every man who has ever served any community for a great length of time, no matter how thorough and efficient the service may have been, and occasional mutterings of discontent were heard; some that he was behind the times, although this was abundantly disproved by the fact that soon after Mr. Whitney left the Iroquois school he passed the specialist examination in classics, and taught successfully in Morrisburg Collegiate Institute till his voluntary resignation in 1893: and some that he was taking too much time in his garden, although it is very probable that his physical ability to do efficient work was kept up by the interesting out-door exercise which this afforded him, as about this time his unceasing work had begun to tell on him physically, especially on his throat, and he was strongly advised by his physician to take a year's rest.

Still, at the last meeting of the Trustees held on October 27th (there were only two meetings that year), attended by the Chairman, Dr. Harkness, and Messrs. Tuttle, Colquhoun, and Carman, Mr. Whitney, on motion of Mr. Tuttle, seconded by Dr. Colquhoun, was reappointed for 1884. Mr. Mills, who was subsequently most active against Mr. Whitney, it will be observed, was absent from this meeting.

The next year the feeling became more acute. Some difficulty had arisen in the school between the headmaster and three or four of the students, one of whom was a son of Mr. Mills, and another of Mr. Tuttle, and the fight became an open one. At the last meeting, held on the 1st of December, at which all the members were present, it was moved by Mr. Mills, seconded by Mr. Carman, that Mr. Whitney be requested to resign, and that the Board advertise for a headmaster at $700 per year. The vote stood: yeas—Mills, Carman and Tuttle; nays—Colquhoun, Robertson and Harkness. The Chairman exercised the right he then possessed of a second vote in case of a tie, and declared the motion lost. A motion by Dr. Colquhoun, seconded by Mr. Robertson, reappointing the old teachers, Mr. Whitney at $800 and Chas. Potter at $500, was then put and carried on the same division, the Chairman again exercising his right to a second vote.

There was no change in the Board the following year, except that Mr. John N. Forward took the place of Dr. Colquhoun, and it was known that Mr. Forward was friendly to the old staff, so as the law then stood, the control of the school in 1885, depended on the selection of the Chairman. In case of a tie in the vote for Chairman, it was provided that the Trustee who was highest on the assessment roll should have the casting vote. As this Trustee was Dr. Harkness it seemed extremely probable that he would be Chairman again; but on the day of the annual meeting Mr. Robertson did not appear; he, it was said, had gone to Ottawa two or three days before the meeting and had not returned. The result was, that on motion of Mr. Carman, seconded by Mr. Tuttle, Mr. Mills was elected Chairman—Harkness and Forward voting nay.

Just about while this was being done the Local Legislature at Toronto so amended the law that the chairman was deprived of his second vote, and the anticipated advantage resulting from a change in the chairmanship did not materialize. In the event of a tie the motion was simply lost, so that if the Trustees stood three and three a dead-lock ensued, unless some one of them gave way. During the year Mr. Robertson died, and was succeeded by Mr. R. M. Bouck, of Irena, who is still a member of the Board.

The meeting to select teachers for the following year was held on December 4th, 1885, all the members being present. A petition headed and circulated by William M. Doran, Reeve, and H. H. Ross, M.A., and very generally signed, asking that the services of Mr. Whitney be retained, was presented, but it was disregarded by the three hostile Trustees, for when it was moved by Dr. Harkness, seconded by John N. Forward, that Mr. Whitney be re-engaged at the old salary, the vote stood: Yeas—Harkness, Forward and Bouck. Nays—Tuttle, Carman and Mills. The motion was, of course lost and the dead-lock seemed imminent, but Mr. Whitney's friends evidently felt that to carry their opposition further might injure the school; besides, no matter how great Mr. Whitney's merits and deserts, they could not hope to get the people to unite in promoting the interests and advancement of the High School so long as the strife over the headmaster continued. At all events, when Mr. Tuttle followed the previous motion with one for the appointment of Mr. James A. Carman at a salary of $900, he found a seconder in Mr. Bouck, and the motion carried without opposition.

Mr. Potter was then reappointed assistant at a salary of $550; but as he held as high a University degree, and had had nearly as much experience in teaching as Mr. Carman, he thought the difference between the salary of the headmaster and assistant too great, and sought and obtained a situation at Newmarket. An effort was then made to engage Mr. Arthur Forward, a Toronto University graduate, but as he had not attended the training school permission could not be obtained from the department, and Mr. A. C. Casselman, a Public School teacher, who held a first-class certificate, was engaged at $550..

This ended all rivalry or want of harmony among the Trustees. The next year the same members were in, the old chairman was reinstated, and thereafter they worked as one man for the upbuilding of the school.

So ends Mr. Whitney's twenty-six years of service—years in which many men who subsequently occupied useful and prominent positions in the community received their education in the Iroquois High School. In it during this period a great deal of thoroughly efficient educational work was done, and judging by the results of the departmental examinations it was never more thorough than in the last two or three years of the period.

At the close of 1893, being in his sixtieth year and having taught fully forty years, he retired from the Morrisburg School, and is now enjoying his well-earned rest in his old home, to which the best wishes and respect of his many friends follow him

CHAPTER XI.

James A. Carman—A New Era—A. C. Casselman—Erection of the New Building—Its Effect on the School—Becomes a Three-Master School—Ralph Ross—The Three C's—J. S. Carstairs—Inspectors' Reports—Increased Attendance—Sources of Revenue.

HEN we last met Mr. James A. Carman he was one of the business men of the village and a Trustee. Very soon after he quit business, being succeeded by his brother, A. B. Carman, and turned his attention to teaching. In April, 1879, he became Principal of the Kemptville High School, then in a backward condition. Under his management it improved rapidly, and in a comparatively short time became one of the best schools in the district. He retired from that in November, 1884, to accompany his wife to Denver, whither she went in search of health. But he had made for himself such a reputation that on his return he was offered several schools, among them the Cornwall High School, where the salary proposed was $1,100, while $900 was all Iroquois could give; but loyalty to his native village, and love for the school his father had founded forty years before, and in which many of his earlier years had been spent, outweighed other considerations, and he determined to cast in his lot with his own people. It may be doubted whether the choice, so far as he was concerned personally, was a wise one, but there can be no two opinions among those familiar with its history, as to its effect on the school. A teacher equally good might, perhaps, have been got, but no other man combined the gifts of teacher and manager possessed by Mr. Carman, with the

JAMES A. CARMAN, B.A.
A. C. CASSELMAN.   JOHN S. CARSTAIRS, B.A.

strong personal influence in the village, that made it possible for the Trustees to get the Council and the people to consent to the expenditure necessary to build and equip the present school.

The Trustees were equally fortunate in the choice of an assistant. Mr. A. C. Casselman, the son of a farmer, was born in the Township of Finch, in the neighboring County of Stormont, on the 26th of June, 1860; entered the Williamstown High School in 1875, where he spent two half-years, working at home in the intervals. After three months in the Morrisburg Collegiate Institute in the early part of 1877, he took his third-class certificate, standing first in the County of Stormont. In 1878 and 1879 he taught at Hainsville, and in the year following again attended the Morrisburg school, and took his second-class certificate, grade A, the only "A" obtained in the school that year. After attending the Normal School at Ottawa, he taught at South Finch until the close of 1883. In 1884 he attended the St. Catharines Collegiate Institute, then under the management of Mr. Seath, now High School Inspector, and in July obtained a first-class, grade C, certificate. From this time until he came to the Iroquois High School he taught a country school, a few miles north of this village, at the place now called Haddo. He was very successful in that school, and made many friends, and from there came to the High School, bringing with him energy, ability, and what was also of some importance, the sympathy and good wishes of a great many people from the country.

It was clear, though, that before much improvement could be expected, something must be done with the building. The Government and County grants, with the fees, had hitherto nearly supported the school, the aid from the village having been very trifling; still this trifle of two or three hundred dollars a year had been grudgingly given, and as the entire cost of a new building, if erected, must fall on the village alone, the possibility of getting the Council or the people to consent to the undertaking seemed hopeless. Still there were favoring conditions. Mr. Wm. M. Doran, who was then Reeve, with the prestige of having the previous year procured the water works at very little cost to the people, was a warm personal friend of Mr. Carman, as well as a friend of the school. The burning of the mill a few years before had been felt in the trade of the village, and the more thoughtful of the people began to realize that should they lose their school, it would be a much greater deprivation, and would probably be permanent. Besides, the Council that year consisted of Messrs. W. L. Redmond, Arthur Patton, Laughlin Cameron and Samuel Larue—all men of experience, with large interests in the village. These, with the buoyant feeling existing at the time, and certain provisions in the law, made the task less difficult than it seemed. The School Board had power, without the consent of the Council, to levy a much larger sum on the village than had ever been exacted, and expend it in increasing the accommodation; and they could ask for all they required to improve the old building or erect a new one, and the Council could refuse only by a two-thirds vote, which, in a Council of five, meant all the members but one. Still they could scarcely avail themselves of their full powers, and would probably not have gone on without a practically unanimous endorsation by the Council.

In the month of April, 1886, the High School Board appointed a deputation to wait on the Council, and a special meeting of that body was called for the 10th of May to receive them. As soon as this was known public interest was aroused. It was understood that Mr. Coulter, an active and somewhat aggressive aspirant for a seat in the Council, intended to oppose the scheme, and it was expected his following would be large, at least among the attendant ratepayers, if not in the Council. When the members of the School Board arrived the chamber in the south-east corner of the Town Hall, where the Council was sitting, was packed to the door. Dr. Harkness and Cephas Mills were to present the case on behalf of the school. The doctor explained that it was impossible to carry on the school successfully without making extensive changes and improvements. These would cost a great deal, and when completed leave them with old and inferior premises, giving them, he thought, less proportionate value for their money than if they put it in an entirely new building. The grants from the Government, which were also the measure of the grants from the Counties, were based largely on building and equipment, and the advantages to be derived from new premises in this respect would be considerable. He expressed a hope that the Council would unite cordially with the Board in making their High School a credit to the place.

Mr. Mills combated the idea that the town would be injured by the necessarily increased taxation. He said no town could hope to make progress where there was not sufficient public spirit to induce the ratepayers to unite in contributing to enterprises that, like this, were clearly conducive to the best interests of the people as a whole, and cited Johnstown, a dilapidated hamlet a few miles to the west, as a sample of a place that hoped to flourish without paying taxes. The crowd was expectant, but gave no sign of approval or disapproval. Mr. Coulter asked a few questions that were readily answered: the venerable clerk, Mr. James Tindale, sen., tried to interject some words of warning, but they fell unheeded, the opposition had melted away. The deputation thanked the Council for the favorable hearing given them and retired, followed soon after by the crowd.

The suitor had declared his love and asked the lady's hand in marriage; she had been coy, but had not refused, he accepted her silence as consent, friends regarded the couple as engaged. What was the lady to do? This was soon settled. The Council acquiesced, and it was

"Moved by A. Patton, seconded by W. L. Redmond, that in view of the fact that our present High School building is entirely inadequate for the present requirements, it being in a very bad state of repair, and in the opinion of the High School Board and this Council it would be very unwise to make the necessary outlay to make it habitable, as the walls are in a condition that would not warrant it; and as the High School Board of Trustees deem a new building necessary, this Council coincide with them and agree unanimously to pass a by-law during the present year to raise by debentures a sufficient amount to pay the same."

This was carried without opposition.

On coming from the meeting Mr. James A. Carman was heard remarking to a friend that the Iroquois Trustees were the broadest, ablest and best High School Board he had ever met.

They had need to be worthy the encomium. They were assuming weighty responsibilities in asking a village with a population not exceeding one thousand, to erect, equip, and— with the help of fees from pupils outside the corporation— maintain a first-class High School. There was in this an implied pledge that it would be well and carefully managed. So far the trust has not been betrayed. The school has, in many respects, surpassed the expectations of its most optimistic friends, and there is now no reason to think that any ratepayer of Iroquois will ever have reason to regret the action then taken.

The contract for the new building was awarded to Mr. Patrick Keefe, on the 17th of September, 1886, at $7,200, though it cost some three or four hundred dollars additional. The plumbing, seating and appliances for heating with hot water added between three and four thousand to this; so the total cost when completed was between $11,000 and $12,000.

Debentures for $7,500 were issued on the 15th of October, 1886, and for $3,000 on March 5th, 1888. On the first issue the principal was made payable in twenty annual instalments, and on the second, in eighteen, and in both cases the interest at 5 per cent. on all remaining unpaid. The annual payments for principal are $541.66. The interest charges were at first, or would have been had the issues been simultaneous, $525 per annum; but being on a descending scale, are now under $300. It will be seen that the amount raised by debentures was not sufficient to meet the full cost of the building, but the balance, as well as what was required

NEW HIGH SCHOOL

for equipment, was taken from the ordinary revenues of the school.

The school soon responded to the efforts being made in its behalf. In 1887, it was found necessary to add a third teacher, and Mr. Ralph Ross, a graduate of Toronto University, was engaged at a salary of $600, which was raised to $700 the following year. This made a strong staff for a three-master school. Casselman had developed a great aptitude for teaching natural science and drawing, while Ross was strong in literature and classics. The school made steady progress, the inspector's reports each year indicating improvement. This continued until the close of 1889, when Mr. Ross, being offered a large increase of salary by the Peterboro' school, resigned just as the school opened in January. The Trustees at once telegraphed Mr. John S. Carstairs, who was then teaching in a Public school in Ottawa, offering him the situation. It was accepted, and the school came under the management of three teachers who were, and continued to be, very warm personal friends, and who delighted in calling themselves the three C.'s—"Carman, Casselman and Carstairs."

Mr. Carstairs was the second son of Robert Carstairs, and was born at Kingston, Ont., May 29th, 1862. His father had, as Sergeant of the 54th Regiment Infantry, spent the earlier part of his life in Ireland, Gibraltar, the West Indies and Quebec, and was at this time foreman in Mowat's bakery—owned by the father of Sir Oliver and Professor Mowat. In 1866, Carstairs began business as baker and confectioner in Iroquois, where the two boys, William and John, attended a private school until the family removed to Arnprior in 1871. Here their business prospered for a time. At ten John S. was the leading boy in the Public school: entered the High School soon after, and in 1876 was the only candidate that passed the December Intermediate Examination. Business troubles now intervened, and in 1879 the family returned to Iroquois. In November of that year John S. entered the Iroquois High School, and in the following May passed the Senior Matriculation of the University of Toronto, and a month later secured a Second-class Certificate and began to teach. During the next eight or ten years he was a principal support of the family, and at the same time continued his studies until he had now passed his third year at the University without attending lectures. He had taught several years in the Public schools in the county, was well known, and had many friends, who welcomed his accession to the High School. Like Mr. Casselman he was in touch with the people in the country, and in that way, aside from his merits as a teacher, was a source of strength to the school. The staff was undoubtedly a good one. Carman's strength lay principally in management and control, and the faculty of implanting in those associated with him, as teachers or students, a desire to excel. Casselman was forceful, energetic, apt to teach, and an enthusiast in the subjects he made his own, while Carstairs was widely read, exact in analysis, clear in exposition, and sympathetic with his pupils. Each appeared to fit in his place, and all worked together in the common interest.

The school had already made great strides towards a front place among High Schools. In 1887 Mr. Seath had reported, "The prospects of the school are excellent, and when it is in the new building it will compare favourably with any other of its size; and also, I note for especial commendation the science master (Mr. Casselman's) teaching of botany. With a properly furnished laboratory the physics and chemistry will, I have no doubt, be equally good." In 1889 Mr. Hodgson said, "I am glad to be able to report that this school is in all respects in a better condition than I have before seen it. The members of the staff are efficient and painstaking, and the pupils seem diligent." He regretted, however, that no provision was made for teaching drill and calisthenics. In 1890 Mr. Seath reported: "This school has improved very much in all respects since I last inspected it;" and in 1891, "This school is in most respects in a very satisfactory condition. The assistants, Mr. Carstairs in particular, have improved very much since my last visit."

The attendance was also continually increasing, and in

1891 the daily average number of pupils was about one hundred. This year also there was a change in the law that materially brightened the prospects of this school.

Hitherto the only assured source of revenue High Schools had were the Legislative grant—an equal amount from the county, and also from the village or town, and fees from the pupils. Anything more was given voluntarily; and, as a rule, had to be provided by the village or town in which the school was situated, which also had to furnish the building and equipments. Our Counties Council had for some time been granting three or four hundred dollars a year more than was required to meet the Legislative grant, still our local assessments were heavy: and in the event of the Counties Council withdrawing this extra grant the school might be seriously crippled. But by the new law it was provided that where the County grant did not bear as great a proportion to the cost of the school, less the Government grant, as the number of pupils from the county bore to that from the village, the county was to give enough additional to make the proportions correspond. That is, the Counties Council has to provide for pupils living in the county outside of the village, while the village provides for its own. Pupils attending from other counties are, however, charged against the village. Under this Act the fees paid by county pupils are fixed by the Counties Council, while those paid by village and non-resident pupils are fixed by the High School Board. Since this law came into operation the grants from the counties—or rather the levies on the counties—have been more than two and a half times greater than the Legislative grants. In 1871 the Government bore about·two-thirds of the cost of the school; in 1881 about one-third, now just one-sixth. Had the law not been so modified as to spread this ever-increasing ratio of local contributions over a wider area it would have been difficult, perhaps impossible, to maintain an efficient High School in a village of the size of Iroquois.

CHAPTER XII.

James A. Carman (*continued*)—Changes—Retirement of Casselman—Four Masters—Criticisms—Newspaper Enterprise—Trouble in the School—Mr. Thompson—Mr. Knox—Mr. Coulter—Election Contest—Retirement of Carman and Carstairs—Death of John A. Carman.

VENTS occurred at the close of 1891 that in a comparatively short period led to an entire change of staff. Mr. Casselman had for some years been giving a good deal of attention to drawing, and with marked success. One pupil, Arthur Shaver, had taken the gold medal in a competition open to the whole Province; and another, Jennie Boyd, had taken the silver medal for a design. The teacher's reputation was such that he was offered the position of Drawing and Writing-master in the Normal School, Toronto, which became vacant about that time. As this was not only more remunerative, but opened a wider field and a brighter prospect, it was accepted. Mr. Carstairs wanted to finish his course in the University, so he asked, and was granted, the first half-year, with the understanding that he might return to the school after taking his degree.

T. K. Sidey, B.A., was engaged to fill Mr. Carstairs' place the first half-year, at $450; and Robert Thompson, a gentleman who had considerable experience as a Public School teacher, succeeded Mr. Casselman. The school was now large for a three-master school, and A. H. Harkness, a student of the school, was engaged to take the drawing class the first half-year, at $125. At the close of that time Miss Ida Dillabough, who is still a member of the staff, was engaged at $500 per year, and the school has since been a four-master school.

There had been few changes in the High School Board since Mr. Carman's appointment as Principal, and such as there were did not affect the relations between the Board and the staff. Mason Mills had succeeded his brother in 1887, and continued in active membership until the close of 1892, being the acting Chairman during the winter of 1891-92, when the Chairman, whose health had been badly shattered, was in Arizona, trying to recuperate. Wm. M. Doran, who was Reeve at the time, succeeded Mr. Tuttle in 1889, but on the passing of the Municipal Amendment Act in that year, disqualifying members of Council, retired, and was succeeded by Dr. Johnston. Under the Act of 1891 the Public School Board acquired the right to appoint a seventh member, and W. L. Redmond, the member of Council who framed the motion to provide for the new building, and who was also Reeve in 1887 and '88, became the seventh member.

To take in the situation fully, it is necessary here to refer to matters outside of the school.

Wm. M. Doran, who had been an influential friend of the school, in close sympathy with Mr. Carman, and had been elected Reeve the fifth time in January, 1891, died suddenly a few weeks later, and was succeeded by Thomas Coulter. This gentleman had good parts, a large personal following, and had been free with his criticisms of the management of the school for several years. He kept a bakery, grocery store and lumber yard, was Secretary of the Public School Board, and held a leading position in the Presbyterian Church; had a son in the Council while his brother-in-law was assessor; so that he was in a position to make his good or ill-will toward the school or the staff a matter of some moment.

Mr. Doran's business had been that of general merchant and dealer in coal and lumber. This latter part was offered for sale a few months after his death, and Mr. Carman became the purchaser, not, as he explained at the time, that he contemplated carrying it on in connection with the school, but he was threatened with deafness, that might unfit him for teaching, so he availed himself of this opportunity to secure a business that would in that event afford him a means of living, the business in the meantime being managed by a friend.

Iroquois had been a rather discouraging field for newspaper enterprise. In 1858 the first newspaper in the county was published here by W. S. Johnston, a former pupil of the Grammar School, an able writer and good practical printer. It was designated the *Iroquois Chief*, and had a considerable circulation; but Mr. Johnston sought a larger town, and removed to Cornwall about the end of its second year. Twenty years later the *Iroquois Times* was tried. This paper had a chequered career. It was first published by a Mr. Graham, who came here from Quebec, but he soon became discouraged, and sold out to Mr. Hendry; who, after a few months' experience, in turn sold to Arthur and Ormond Brouse, grandsons of the George Brouse who figures prominently early in the history of the school. A couple of years later it was leased to R. D. Harkness, the present proprietor of the *St. Lawrence News*, for a year. At the end of that time, in July, 1882, the plant was taken to the North-West. In 1888, B. C. Beach, a son of M. F. Beach, commenced the publication of the *St. Lawrence News*. He soon secured a fairly good circulation, and the venture gave promise of success, but the publisher had little taste for writing, and from the first was assisted in this department by members of the High School staff. Soon after Mr. Carstairs had graduated and again taken up his work in the school, Mr. Beach decided to "go west," and offered to let or sell the paper. Partly because of a desire to retain the paper in the place, and partly because he liked newspaper work, Mr. Carstairs formed a partnership with a R. A. McLelland, who was then manager of a branch of the Union Bank, doing business here, and leased the paper for three years.

In the meantime the school had not been running as smoothly as usual. Mr. Thompson had been developing some eccentricities of character, and had succeeded in getting himself arraigned before the Police Magistrate for striking one of the boys. The Principal and the Trustees defended him vigorously, not, they said, because they approved of what he had done, but in order to maintain the discipline of the school. The affair was settled without a conviction, and if there was any more friction inside the school it was not brought to the knowledge of the general public. However, Mr. Carman appears to have been disappointed in his assistant, and near the close of the year recommended a change.

When the Board decided to act on the recommendation, Mr. Carstairs suggested that an effort be made to secure Robert Hunter Knox, whom he assigned a first place among the young men who came within the sphere of his observation while in Toronto the previous winter. This gentleman was at once communicated with, and soon after engaged, and his work in the school since has fully borne out what was then said in his behalf. Now that the people interested know both men as they were then known to Mr. Carstairs, nothing could more strikingly vindicate the action then taken than the mere suggestion that the present Science-master should give place to his predecessor.

Nevertheless, no teacher that ever was in the school appeared to have more partisans than Mr. Thompson. He had been an active worker in the Presbyterian Sunday School, and had thus secured the goodwill of the people of that faith. His wife was a charming woman, and had made many friends. A petition in his behalf was circulated in the school by a son of Mr. Coulter and very generally signed by the students. Still, it is probable that his dismissal was the occasion, rather than the cause, of the efforts being made to embarrass the Trustees.

There had for several years been a party in the village more or less opposed to the school as conducted. They had been so accustomed to having their children educated almost free of cost to themselves, either as individuals or ratepayers, that they resented the changed conditions under which the burdens were more equitably distributed. Mr. Coulter, the Reéve, notwithstanding he had as a member of the Counties Council been instrumental in abolishing fees, thus putting the whole cost of maintenance on the taxpayers, was the recognized leader of this party. He and his friends had found so much fault with the management that early in October, Mr. A. B. Carman resigned the position of Secretary, which he had efficiently filled for five years, and retired from the High School Board, that no charge of nepotism might lie at his door.

Mr. Coulter soon after aired his grievances in the local paper, and advocated petitioning the Legislature to deprive the Counties of any representation on the Board. He contended that all the Trustees should be appointed by the village authorities. As the village already had four-sevenths of the representation, and bore little more than one-third of the cost of maintaining the school, the proposition seemed scarcely reasonable.

A second letter, written a short time before the elections, was more skilfully worded, and was aimed first at the Chairman, because he lived outside of the village and received his appointment from the Counties Council; but was largely a personal attack on the members of the staff and Board within the village that were considered most vulnerable. Mr. Mills, out of whose store some of the furnishings of the school had been procured, was described as "Sutler" to the School Board; and it was rather broadly stated that the school was suffering because Mr. Carstairs and Mr. Carman were giving too much attention to private business, the latter gentleman being designated the "Head of the Coal Combine."

This called forth rejoinders. That from Mr. Carstairs, who wields a caustic pen, was regarded as rather severe; but Mr. Carman's simply set forth his relations to the school, explained the circumstances attending his becoming the owner of the coal and lumber business, pointed to what had been done by the fathers of the present generation, and asked their sons not to "fly at each other's throats" at the bidding of Mr. Coulter, notwithstanding he was, for the time being, Reeve of the village. Both, however, intimated that so soon as it was made manifest that the people thought they were not giving value for what they were receiving, their connection with the school would cease.

This was the position in which the respective parties stood at the time of the municipal election. A day or two after nomination it was found that all the nominees for councillors had withdrawn but four, who were thus practically elected by acclamation. Adam Harkness had not been at the meeting, but had been nominated as Reeve in opposition to Mr. Coulter. He had had a somewhat extended experience in connection with municipal affairs in the Township of Matilda, was Postmaster of the village, had interested himself a good deal in the School and Mechanics' Institute, and was regarded as not personally objectionable to the people in the village otherwise than that he was not in accord politically with the majority. However, it was thought by the friends of the school that as the political complexion of the Council was already firmly fixed, and could not be affected seriously by the admission of one of the opposite cult, and that by his standing for election a fair expression of public opinion might be obtained on this matter of greatest interest to the people, the consent of Mr. Harkness was sought and obtained, and the election was fought out, nominally at least on the school question, and resulted in the return of Mr. Coulter.

At the first meeting of the new Council the name of Mr. Mills was dropped from the list of Trustees, and that of Edward McNulty, a leading supporter of Mr. Coulter's, substituted. Ostensibly the verdict had been against the school and the staff, though it is extremely doubtful if a direct vote on the one question would have resulted in the same way. Mr. Carman and his friends, believing in the loyalty of the people to their school, did not take sufficient account of other faiths and prejudices equally deep-seated. A broad and liberal-minded man himself, he could not sympathize with or measure the feelings of many of his own friends, though a study of the history of the village and the school might have taught him the lesson. He could not understand why it was regarded as necessary to think alike on all national questions to enable us to work together for our local interests. He forgot that Mr. Carstairs himself, a somewhat pronounced Conservative, was a sort of innovation in the school, and that Mr. Knox was coming on his recommendation. Still, he had asked the people for their verdict; it had been given, and he felt that it was not for him to cavil about the way in which the result had been reached. Neither he nor Mr. Carstairs had sought the school; they could now only remain in it by, in a measure, forfeiting their self-respect, and they decided, notwithstanding the desire of the Board to retain their services, to retire at the close of the Academic year. The school never was more flourishing. It had been raised in seven years from a small two-master school until now it stood among the first High Schools in the Province. The four men who, as teachers, had been mainly instrumental in bringing this about were Carman, Casselman, Carstairs and Ross. Their work in the school was done, but they were leaving a record that could not fail to provoke to emulation their successors, and lead to continued effort to maintain the reputation and standing of the institution.

The resignation of Mr. Carstairs was presented at a meeting of the High School Board held on June 30th, 1893, the members present being Dr. Harkness, Chairman, Messrs. A. J. Ross, E. McNulty and J. N. Forward, when it was moved by A. J. Ross, seconded by E. McNulty, and carried:

"That J. S. Carstairs' resignation be accepted, and that the Board take this occasion to express their regret at the severance of his connection with the school, as well as their entire satisfaction with his services. They also desire to express their hope for his success in whatever calling he may decide to pursue."

Mr. Carman's was presented at a meeting held on August 1st, the members present being the chairman and Messrs. J. N. Forward, R. M. Bouck, W. L. Redmond, N. G. Sherman, E.

McNulty and A. J. Ross, when it was moved by Mr. Bouck, seconded by Mr. Forward, and carried:

"That the Board, in accepting Mr. Carman's resignation, wish to express their regret that anything should have transpired in High School affairs that should cause him to tender his resignation. We are aware that the school loses a head whose place, we believe, will be hard to fill. The growth of the school under his leadership has been great, and in a large measure is due to his untiring efforts in its behalf. We trust that although he is severing his connection with the school as a leader he will still remain a resident of the village, and that the school will receive the benefit of his counsel in assisting the Board to maintain the high position the school has gained under his able leadership."

Just three weeks after the struggle in the Town Hall, that resulted in severing the connection of James A. Carman with the school, his father, John A. Carman, passed to his rest. Forty-six years before, in the vigor of his early manhood, he had founded the school. For years he watched over and assisted it in its early struggles. During the whole of his subsequent life he regarded it with an interest born of the sacrifices he had made in its behalf. Now, in the evening of his days, he had the satisfaction of seeing his son, in a different way, and under different circumstances, repeat the story of his earlier years. It seems almost a pity that he also lived to witness what must have seemed to him an act of ingratitude on the part of those whom he had striven so hard to benefit. But he had the consciousness of having done what he could, and what he believed to be right, and we have no reason to doubt his faith in the beneficence of the ultimate results. He was not only the principal, but the last of the original friends and benefactors of the school.

On the day after his death the Board met, and on motion of Mr. Mills, seconded by W. L. Redmond, passed the following resolution:

"The High School Board, of Iroquois, having heard with deep regret of the death of John A. Carman, the founder and benefactor of the school, who, by his generosity, donated the first building, and who for many years was a Trustee, desire to convey their sincere sympathy to the wife and relations of the deceased in their dark hour of tribulation, and that the Secretary be hereby requested to convey to Mrs. Carman and family a copy of this resolution.

"The Board further orders that the school be closed to-morrow to allow the teachers and scholars to attend the funeral of the founder in a body."

This closes an epoch in the school, in many respects the most brilliant in its history. The three men most intimately associated with it are now widely separated, but we have abundant evidence that they all look back with pleasure and some degree of pride to the time when they were working together with a common purpose in the Iroquois High School.

Mr. Carman, whose wife had found it necessary to spend some previous winters in a less rugged climate, moved to Denver soon after his retirement from the school, and is likely to make that city his permanent home.

Mr. Carstairs spent his first year, after leaving here, in Toronto, writing for the press and studying law, but has now been for a year and a half Headmaster of the Stirling High School.

Mr. Casselman is now not only Writing and Drawing-master in the Normal School, but Examiner in Drawing and Lecturer on Drawing in the School of Pedagogy. He is also author of the High School Drawing Course, which is not only used in Ontario, but in the other provinces of the Dominion. Mr. J. L. Hughes, senior Inspector of Public Schools for the city of Toronto, says that it is the best book that has been authorized by the Department on any subject for many years.

PRESENT STAFF.

CHAPTER XIII.

"Men may come and men may go,
But I go on forever."

Joseph A. Jackson—New Regime—Mr. Knox—Miss Hare—Miss Ross—
Mr. Warren—Miss Dillabough—Continued Progress—Present Board
—Dr. Harkness—R. M. Bouck—Howard Durant—J. N. Forward
—N. G. Sherman—Edward McNulty—Headmasters and Assistants—Revenues and Salaries—General Results—New Features.

ISS DILLABOUGH at this time withdrew from the school to finish her course as a specialist at Toronto University, and it thus became necessary to secure a new Principal and two assistants. Notices in the *Globe* and *Mail* brought in some fifty or sixty applications. After wrestling for several hours with these, the Trustees finally appointed Joseph A. Jackson Headmaster, with a salary of $1,000; Miss Zella Hare Mathematical-master, at $600; and Miss Nellie Ross, at $500; these, with Mr. Knox, Science-master, constituting the new staff.

Mr. Jackson was of English parentage. His father, the son of a banker in Newcastle-on-Tyne, was fairly well educated, but, not succeeding in the Old Country, he came to Canada about the close of the Crimean War, settled in the Township of Edwardsburg, married, and became a Public School teacher. In 1872 he died, leaving a widow with five children, of whom Joseph A. was the eldest, being then almost twelve years of age. His mother, having been a seamstress before her marriage, now resorted to that as a means of livelihood, and started a small tailoring establishment at Ventnor, and her eldest son divided his time between working in a shingle mill, going to school, and learning to cut for his mother, whose business was increasing. When about eighteen he was, through the influence of a young school teacher, named Beaman, induced to turn his attention to that profession. In July, 1879, he passed the entrance examination to the High School. Not being in very good health, he became discouraged, and determined to return to his trade of cutting, and, with that end in view, came to Iroquois to enter Mr. A. B. Carman's shop. Here he met Mr. James A. Carman, who "laughed him out of the blues," and induced him to go to the Kemptville High School, of which Mr. Carman was then Headmaster. He commenced there in January, 1880, and the following summer got his Third-class Certificate. After attending the Model School, at Athens, he taught the balance of that year and the whole of the next. In January, 1882, he returned to the Kemptville school, and again, at the end of the half-year, advanced a step, taking a Second-class Certificate. He then taught until September, 1883, when ill-health compelled him to desist. Again, he made up his mind to abandon teaching, and established a tailoring business in Cardinal, but a few months later left that with his brother, who had been his partner, and in September, 1884, entered Cobourg Collegiate Institute, where he matriculated in June, 1885, and in 1889 graduated from Victoria University, with First-class honors in Metaphysics, Logic, and Civil Polity. He taught in Gananoque High School until the close of that year, when he went as Classical-master to Kemptville, where he remained a year and a half, returning to Gananoque in 1891, and continuing there until appointed Headmaster here. He was rather late in beginning, but he has pushed on rapidly, and is making a good record in Iroquois.

Robert Hunter Knox was born of Scottish parents in the Town of St. Mary's, in 1868. When but eleven years of age he passed the necessary examination, and entered the St. Mary's Collegiate Institute. At fifteen he took his Third-class non-Professional; at sixteen, his Second-class, and at seventeen, matriculated. He then attended the Model School, and taught in a Public School two or three years. In 1889, he entered Toronto University, and graduated in Arts in 1892, taking First-class honors all around in the department of Natural Science, specializing the last year in Geology and related subjects. During 1891 he taught for a short time in Georgetown High School, and Ridgetown Collegiate Institute, and in 1892 in Jarvis Street Collegiate Institute, Toronto. Though he may have inherited the scientific bent from his father, who was a stonemason and builder, the tendency to intellectual pursuits, characteristic of the family, appears to have been derived from the mother, whose grandfather, Robert Hunter, was an Independent minister. Her father served as a regular soldier in the 90th Regiment before he came to this country, and was captain of a company during the troubles of 1837. She herself was a school teacher, as was also her brother. Her two daughters—one of whom, Agnes Knox, has won fame as an elocutionist—were both teachers, while her three sons, Robert Hunter, Andrew A., and William John, are all specialists in science, the first at Iroquois High School, the second at Chatham Collegiate Institute, and the third at Orangeville High School.

Miss Hare and Miss Ross were both graduates of Toronto University. The former taught mathematics, bookkeeping, drawing and writing, while the latter took English literature, grammar and modern languages. Both of these ladies came from the western part of the province, Miss Ross being a daughter of the Hon. G. W. Ross, Minister of Education.

Some little trepidation was felt about the large representation of young ladies on the staff. Still the school went on fairly well. It was visited by Mr. Hodgson in October, who reported: "This school is in a very satisfactory condition; good work is being done in all the departments."

However, when the year closed, both ladies tendered their resignations, and Mr. James M. Warren, of Hamilton, a specialist in mathematics, and Miss Ida Dillabough, who had already proved her worth in the school, were appointed to the vacant places.

Mr. Warren was born in Hamilton, in November, 1872, and eleven years afterwards passed his entrance examination, and entered the Hamilton Collegiate Institute. In 1886 he obtained a Second-class Certificate, and in 1888 a First-class C., and the following year matriculated with honors in Mathematics, Botany and Chemistry. In 1890 he obtained a First-class B. non-Professional, and graduated in 1893 from Toronto University. During his first two years at the university he obtained First-class honors in Mathematics, and during the last the same in theoretical and practical Physics; attended the School of Pedagogy from October, 1893, to May, 1894, and obtained while there a Second-class Professional Certificate with honors, and also an interim Certificate as specialist in Mathematics with honors.

Miss Dillabough is the daughter of Mr. Lawrence Dillabough, of Dundela. After passing the entrance, she attended the Morrisburg Collegiate Institute until she took a First-class non-Professional Certificate. She then went to the School of Pedagogy at Kingston and got her Professional, after which she taught a year and a half in Norwood High School before coming to Iroquois in 1892. After teaching one year here, she withdrew to take a course as specialist in the modern languages—German and French.

The staff is undoubtedly a strong one, all the members being in the vigor of early manhood and womanhood, and all putting forth strenuous efforts to maintain and improve the standing of the school. These are being warmly seconded by the Trustees, who are continually adding to the equipment, especially in the science department and library. In September, 1894, Mr. Seath, the Inspector, said: "The science equipment of this school is remarkably good, a result which is evidently due to the energy and enthusiasm of the Science-master. A good spirit of work pervades all the school, and its general tone is satisfactory."

On the occasion of his next visit in March, 1895, he reported:

DR. HARKNESS, *Chairman.*
R. M. BOUCK.　　　　　　　　　　JOHN N. FORWARD.
　　　　　　N. G. SHERMAN.
H. C. DURANT.　　　　　　　EDWARD McNULTY, *Secretary.*

"The organization has been much improved since my last visit. The equipment of this school, especially in science, is unusually good. There are exceedingly few schools in the Province in which in science there is the same excellent spirit and enthusiasm. The condition of the laboratory and the museum is highly creditable to Mr. Knox."

The present Board of Trustees is composed of six members: Dr. John Harkness, Chairman, R. M. Bouck, Howard Durant, J. N. Forward, N. G. Sherman, and Edward McNulty, the latter gentleman being Secretary and Treasurer. The first three are appointees of the Counties Council, and the remaining three of the Village Council. The Public School Board of the village should have appointed a seventh, but that body, being composed of six members, divided evenly, and, as neither party would yield, and no compromise could be obtained, no appointment was made.

To those who have followed me, no further reference to the Chairman is now necessary. Mr. Bouck is also an old member, having been first appointed in October, 1885. In early life he was a school teacher, and was for a time Principal of the Public School in the village. Later, he turned his attention to farming in the Township of Matilda, and was also for several years a member of the Township Council. He has given a good deal of attention to school matters, and is an efficient Trustee.

When A. B. Carman retired, in 1892, A. J. Ross was appointed in his place, and became Secretary-Treasurer; but, in 1893, the Mountain members of the Council claimed a Trustee, and William Marshall, a gentleman supporting and very much interested in the school, was appointed. At the close of that year he retired, and was succeeded by Mr. Durant. Mr. Durant is a young merchant of the village of Inkerman, and may be regarded as the representative on the Board of the Township of Mountain. This is his first year, and he has as yet taken very little part in the affairs of the school.

Mr. Forward is at present the oldest member except the Chairman, having been appointed a few months before Mr.

Bouck. About thirty-five years ago he married the youngest daughter of the late Peter Carman, and has since been a resident of this village. He kept store for a time, but in recent years has devoted his attention principally to fruit raising, gardening, and we might add music, though this latter has been almost entirely for the love of it. He has for a great many years led the choir in the Methodist Church, and in Mr. Whitney's time gave lessons in the High School. Two of his sons matriculated from the school: the eldest, Arthur, graduating some time after, and being now a practising barrister in the City of Ottawa. He has been a good friend of the school, always ready to hold up the hands of the master so long as he felt that he was endeavoring to perform his part.

Nelson G. Sherman was born in the Township of Oznabruck nearly seventy years ago, and came to this place just as it was taking form as a village, and commenced business as a carriage-maker. For over forty years he has been one of our foremost business men, and during the greater part of that time was a member of the Public School Board. He was also several years in the Council, but never took part in the affairs of the High School until 1893, when, being Chairman of the Public School Board, he was appointed to represent that body as a Trustee of the High School. This year it was feared the Public School Trustees would not agree, so the Council deferred making their appointment until it became clear that Mr. Sherman would not retain his seat if not appointed by the Council.

Edward McNulty came to Iroquois with his father when very young, and was educated at the Public and High Schools here. When a mere lad he entered the store of C. & M. Mills, and remained with the firm for several years, first as clerk in their store, and afterwards as manager of branch stores at Cardinal and Prescott. Nearly twenty years ago he commenced business here on his own account, and has now one of the two largest stores in the village. Since his appointment he has interested himself very much in the school, makes an efficient Secretary-Treasurer, has progressive ideas, and has shown that he will perform his part towards maintaining and improving the standing and reputation of the institution.

The following list of the names of Headmasters and their assistants, with the salaries received in each case, marks the changes in the school, and is not a bad indication of the progress made during the period:

```
1880—William A. Whitney, Principal..... $800 00
      Alexander McLeod, Assistant......  400 00
                                              ————$1,200 00
1881—William A. Whitney, Principal ....  $800 00
      John M. Kinney, B.A., Assistant...  400 00
                                              ———— 1,200 00
1882—William A. Whitney, Principal ....  $800 00
      William Montgomery, Assistant ....  400 00
                                              ———— 1,200 00
1883—William A. Whitney, Principal ....  $800 00
      William Montgomery, Assistant ....  500 00
                                              ———— 1,300 00
1884—William A. Whitney, Principal ....  $800 00
      Wm. Montgomery, 1st half-year ..⎫
      Chas. Potter, B.A., 2nd half-year.⎭  500 00
                                              ———— 1,300 00
1885—William A. Whitney, Principal ....  $800 00
      Chas. Potter, B.A., Assistant......  500 00
                                              ———— 1,300 00
1886—James A. Carman, Principal ......  $900 00
      A. C. Casselman, Assistant ........  550 00
                                              ———— 1,450 00
1887—James A. Carman, Principal ......$1,000 00
      A. C. Casselman, Assistant ........    600 00
      Ralph Ross, B.A., As't 2nd half-year 300 00
                                              ———— 1,900 00
1888—James A. Carman, Principal ......$1,000 00
      A. C. Casseman, Assistant ........    650 00
      Ralph Ross, Assistant ............    700 00
                                              ———— 2,350 00
1889—James A. Carman, Principal ......$1,000 00
      A. C. Casselman, Assistant ........    700 00
      Ralph Ross, Assistant ............    700 00
                                              ———— 2,400 00
```

1890—James A. Carman, Principal $1,000 00
    A. C. Casselman, Assistant 700 00
    J. S. Carstairs, Assistant.......... 700 00
    ———————$2,400 00

1891—James A. Carman, Principal $1,000 00
    A. C. Casselman, Assistant 700 00
    J. S. Carstairs, Assistant 700 00
    ——————— 2,400 00

1892—James A. Carman, Principal $1,000 00
    T. K. Sidey, Assistant, 1st half..... 450 00
    J. S. Carstairs, Assistant, 2nd half.. 400 00
    Robert Thompson, Assistant 675 00
    A. H. Harkness, Assistant, 1st half.. 125 00
    Ida Dillabough Assistant, 2nd half.. 250 00
    ——————— 2,900 00

1893—Jas. A. Carman, Principal, 1st half } $1,000 00
    J. A. Jackson, Principal, 2nd half }
    R. H. Knox, Assistant............ 800 00
    J. S. Carstairs, Assistant, 1st half .. 400 00
    Miss Zella Hare, Assistant, 2nd half 300 00
    Miss Dillabough, Assistant, 1st half } 500 00
    Miss Nellie Ross, Assistant, 2nd half }
    ——————— 3,000 00

1894—J. A. Jackson, Principal..........$1,000 00
    R. H. Knox, Assistant 800 00
    Miss Zella Hare, Assistant, 1st half.. 300 00
    James Warren, Assistant, 2nd half.. 350 00
    Miss Nellie Ross, Assistant, 1st half. 250 00
    Miss Dillabough, Assistant, 2nd half 300 00
    ——————— 3,000 00

1895—J. A. Jackson, Principal..........$1,000 00
    R. H. Knox, Assistant............ 875 00
    James Warren, Assistant 800 00
    Miss Dillabough, Assistant, 1st half.. } 600 00
    *Miss H. A. Snider, M.A., Asst., 2nd half }
    ——————— 3,275.00

A continuation of the statement of revenue that appeared in an earlier chapter not only serves the same purpose, but also illustrates rather strikingly one phase of the transition

---

* Miss Snider was engaged temporarily, to give Miss Dillabough a rest.

from a voluntary school assisted by the State to a purely State school, fitting into our educational system.

YEAR.	LEGIS- LATIVE GRANT.	COUNTY GRANTS.		VILLAGE GRANT.	FEES.	TOTAL.
		To meet Legislative Grant.	Maintenance.			
1881	$576 30	$650 00	......	$200 00	$73 00	$1499 30
1882	541 15	650 00	......	200 00	58 00	1449 15
1883	511 61	650 00	......	200 00	54 00	1415 61
1884	504 00	650 00	......	350 00	86 00	1590 00
1885	500 00	650 00	......	300 00	92 00	1542 00
1886	468 30	650 00	......	800 00	125 00	2043 30
1887	451 81	1010 00	......	1200 00	283 50	2945 31
1888	592 52	900 00	......	1000 00	377 25	2869 77
1889	716 06	1000 00	......	1000 00	412 50	3128 56
1890	709 63	1100 00	......	1000 00	439 30	3248 93
1891	691 31	1100 00	$898 85	900 00	*307 50	3889 66
1892	674 82	750 00	1150 00	1500 00	......	4074 82
1893	712 74	725 00	1300 00	1500 00	†33 00	4270 74
1894	690 46	725 00	1476 60	1500 00	‡245 00	4637 06

* First half-year. † Non-resident. ‡ Non-resident and last half-year.

By comparing the total revenue with the salaries paid teachers during the eight years ending in 1894, it will be seen that the former exceeds the latter by nearly $9,000, or about $1,100 a year. This is due in large measure to expenditure on building, equipment, and the enlargement of the school grounds. There has been no separate capital account kept, so that, except the debentures for $10,500, everything is included in the statement given. The building cost some $1,200 or $1,500 more than provided for by debentures. There has been expended on the Library, the fitting up and furnishing of a Science-room and Museum in the basement, and a Gymnasium on the third flat, at least $2,000 more; and in 1891 a quarter of an acre was added to the school grounds at a cost of $600, and it was further swelled over $200 by the imposition of fees by the Counties Council in June, 1894, that were not taken into account when the estimates for that year were made, thus leaving the actual cost of maintenance, outside of teachers' salaries, about $600 a year

Of course, some of this expenditure for equipment was charged against the village alone, but there is a pretty wide borderland between what is clearly for building and equipment and what for maintenance. And in view of the efforts put forth by the village to provide first-class accommodation, it has been the practice with those having to do with the financial affairs of the school to draw the dividing line as near to actual building and equipment as is permissible.

The cost of an educational institution is a very good measure of the efforts put forth to reach the end desired, but the results of the work done by the teachers are too impalpable, too elusive, to be subjected to exact analysis or counted in figures. We know an effort is being made to do this, and the outcome may be of value, but the system has, until very recently, been in a state of flux, and any attempt to estimate from this the character of the work done over a long period might be very misleading. We will, therefore, content ourselves with giving a few more figures bearing on the attendance and cost per pupil, and taken from the report filed in the Education Department and from the accounts of the school. The years 1863, 1873, and so on, have been selected because they are the only equidistant years for which the data were available.

Year.	Number of Pupils.	Salaries of Masters.	Total Revenue.	Paid in Salaries for each Pupil.	Other Expenses per Pupil.	Total Cost per Pupil.
1863	70	$800 00	$843 47	$11 42	$0 62	$12 04
1873	112	1200 00	1541 59	10 71	3 05	13 76
1883	60	1200 00	1450 61	20 00	4 17	24 17
*1893	172	2900 00	4074 82	16 86	6 83	23 69

* From the report of 1893, but the figures given are for 1892.

The number of pupils given is, we believe, in each case the whole number in attendance during the year. The average daily attendance would probably be about one-third less.

In recent years "physical culture" has become a marked feature of the school. So recently as 1889, Inspector Hodgson regretted that no provision was made for teaching drill or calisthenics. Very soon after that a gymnasium was fitted up on the third floor, and a regular system of exercise and drill instituted. Dumb-bells, Indian clubs, wands and the various other devices intended to conduce to bodily vigor have come to be regarded as being nearly, if not altogether, as essential to the proper equipment of a High School as blackboards, maps and lexicons. At the annual "Commencements," the exhibitions of skill in the use of these appliances have, for some years, been regarded as among the most pleasing features of these entertainments. Since the advent of Mr. Knox, the present Science-master, more attention has been paid to outdoor sports and games. No day in the calendar of the school is looked forward to with more eagerness by the pupils than the annual meet of the High School Athletic Association. For days, sometimes for weeks, before it takes place the prizes, contributed by the business men of the village and friends of the students, are exhibited in the windows of one of the shops, and wistfully scanned by the prospective possessors.

These contests and games are so arranged that every pupil in the school may find a place adapted to his physical capacities and peculiarities. They consist principally of foot and bicycle races, jumping in its various forms, vaulting, throwing weights, such as the shoulder stone and caber, and games of ball and lacrosse. They are modelled somewhat after the Olympian and other Grecian games, and it is hoped their influence on the character and conduct of the people may be as salutary as that attributed to their great prototypes. Nor have we reason to think otherwise. The Greeks, and the Romans as well, owe the place they fill in history as much to their physical as to their mental superiority. Their games and their literature were intertwined, and many of their greatest intellectual efforts were put forth in behalf of strength, endurance and courage. Had there been no Achilles or Hector, would there have been a Homer? When the circus, with its hired or barbarian athletes, took the place of the contests among the freemen, the decline of these nations had begun. It is the same with our own race and nation; its supremacy is largely the outcome of its fighting qualities. If the tap of its morning drum continuously heralds the rising sun, it is because of the pluck and energy born of muscular effort. In a new country, where the conditions of life conduce to bodily vigor, the want of physical training in the schools may not be felt, but we think the new departure has been taken none too soon. So far the boys who are foremost in the sports are among the foremost in their classes, and the added labor or exercise appears to be rather a help than a hindrance to their progress in the ordinary work of the school.

In addition to the annual games, other sports claim the attention of the students, such as skating and hockey in the winter, and baseball, lacrosse and football in the summer. This last is the favorite just now. The "team" consists of eleven players, and is a strong one. It has met and vanquished nearly all the teams from surrounding villages and towns, and is now regarded as the champion team of Eastern Ontario: that is, of all the country from Kingston east to the Province line.

Another new and very commendable feature in the working of the school is the Science lectures. These owe their origin mainly to Mr. Knox, but he has been well seconded by the other members of the staff and the Chairman of the Board of Trustees. They are intended not only for the students in the school, but for all who will take interest enough to attend. They were begun in the winter of 1893-94 by inducing local men familiar with special departments of knowledge to prepare and deliver lectures in the Assembly-room. Some of these were very interesting and instructive, and attracted considerable attention. As time went on the circle was widened, and scientists were brought in from other towns and villages, and from Ottawa and Toronto. Special efforts have been made to interest the farmers, and experts in agriculture,

horticulture and dairying, have been secured. At the last meeting lectures by C. C. James, M.A., Deputy Minister of Agriculture for Ontario, and Professor Robertson, Dominion Dairy Commissioner, were given in the Town Hall to a very large audience.

These lectures are under the auspices of the Natural Science Association, which has also organized weekly Saturday excursions through the country during the summer season for the study of natural history and the collection of specimens for their museum, which is now the second best High School museum in the Province of Ontario.

CHAPTER XIV.

The Alumni.

 SCHOOL is like a world in miniature, unchanging forces operating from generation to generation on similar material produce but slightly varying results, yet the individual changes follow each other in rapid succession. Fifty years is a very short period in the world's history, or even in the life of a nation, but the men and women of fifty years ago, where are they? Those who have succeeded them are, nevertheless, actuated by the same motives, the same desires, and the same ambitions. What the half-century accomplishes in the larger field, four or five years will do in the smaller. Indeed, it is doubtful if the average school life of the pupil is more than half of that, so the men and women who owe a part of their intellectual development to the Iroquois School may be numbered by many hundreds, perhaps by thousands. Of the lives of a few of these we have had glimpses by the way as we traced the history of the school; those of a few others fairly representative of the students may be of interest. In sketching them we shall confine ourselves to the earlier students, those whose life work is well on its way, perhaps ended, merely premising that what we may say will be almost entirely from personal recollection.

Among those who entered the school when first opened were some half dozen youths who appear to have made some progress in the higher branches before entering, probably with Mr. Kerr, who had taught in the common school. They were: James Ault, Ormond Skinner, Rufus Carman, Philip and William Keeler, and Cyrus Brouse. Each of these boys was the pride and hope of the family to which he belonged. The three first named were frequently referred to during the speechmaking that was then, as now, common at donation parties and socials, as living evidences of the success of the school and intelligence of the citizens. Ault and Skinner studied medicine, and graduated from McGill College about 1854. Except Dr. Wm. H. Brouse, who graduated some years earlier, and was practising in Prescott, they were the first native doctors in this county. Ault practised at Dixon's Corners for a short time, and then left for newer and better fields. He returned to Iroquois some years later, and died at his mother's, the old Simon Ault homestead, in the eastern part of the village, in 1867. Skinner went to Western Ontario, and succeeded in getting a very good practice in a small town near Hamilton. He, too, died early. Rufus Carman adopted the legal profession, and was the first native lawyer. He remained in Iroquois for several years, and, when the village was incorporated, was appointed Clerk. He also has joined the silent majority. The Keeler boys, sons of old Squire Keeler, were bright lads, but, especially William, the younger, a little trying to the school authorities. Neither of them graduated; some youthful escapade drove William from the school and from home. He went West, and subsequently joined an American surveying party, became an engineer, got employment with the Government, and died at Washington some twenty or more years ago. Philip did business for a time at Dixon's Corners and South Mountain; realized on a large farm his father had deeded to him to enable him to vote, and left the country with considerable money nearly forty years ago. I believe he, too, is long since dead. The last of "that bright band," Mr. Brouse, has had a chequered career. First, as a druggist in St. Catharines; then as a farmer with his father, Mr. Jacob Brouse; later, in the gold mines of British Columbia, where he made and lost a fortune.; again, as a farmer on the old homestead; and he is now trying to wrest fortune, or at least the means of subsistence, from a farm not far from the city of Winnipeg.

Very few of the students of that time turned their attention to school teaching. Among the young men we only remember Mr. J. S. Rattray; and of the ladies, Miss Emily Coons, now Mrs. Silas Redmond; and Miss Charlotte Parlow, now Mrs. N. M. Davy.

Among the students in the school a few years later, or about 1852, was a small lad, the eldest son of an itinerant Methodist Episcopal minister, who was stationed here at the time, and who afterwards chose to spend the evening of his days in this village. This lad has since been closely identified with the educational interests of this county, and is one of the four or five we have selected for more extended notices.

Arthur Brown was born in South Crosby, County of Leeds, May 13th, 1840. His grandfather, William Brown, had served in the war of 1812, and at Prescott. The clerical instinct in the family must have been strong, for notwithstanding he was a Methodist and a soldier, he was designated "Priest Brown." His eldest son, William, was a most devoted minister in the Church of his choice, and died here a few years ago universally regretted. Arthur was again the eldest son, and entered this school during Mr. Dick's time, when about twelve years old. He remained in the school two years, when the family removed to Farmersville, now Athens. There being no Grammar School there at that time, he attended the common school until he obtained a certificate to teach, and began teaching in Mallorytown in 1857. He attended the Belleville Seminary in 1858 and 1859. In the latter year Mr. Carman, who had been Professor of Mathematics from the time he entered the school, became Principal. Later Mr. Brown spent some time in the Farmersville Grammar School, first as student and then as teacher, and continued teaching, mostly in Public Schools, until January, 1874, when he came to Morrisburg and assumed the management of the *Morrisburg Herald*, a Liberal local paper which was about being started, and the first issue of which was published on the 24th of

March following. He still continued to give a great deal of attention to educational matters, and when in 1878, Rev. Mr. Ferguson, on account of his advanced age, retired from the position of Inspector of Public Schools for the County, Mr. Brown was unanimously chosen by the Counties Council as his successor. His career since has fully justified the confidence then so strikingly expressed by the Council. He has devoted his whole attention to the schools of this county for nearly twenty years, and is regarded, and justly so, as one of the best inspectors in the Province. Educationally, this county is far in advance of any other eastern county, and well abreast of any county east or west. This is, no doubt, to a considerable extent due to the character of the people. Nevertheless, Mr. Brown has contributed largely to the results obtained.

Our own recollections of many who were contemporaries of Mr. Brown at the Grammar School are still somewhat vivid: His younger brother, Miles Brown, now practising medicine at Chesterville; Edwin Brouse, who, after graduating in medicine, went to British Columbia with his brother, Cyrus, returned later and practised in Brockville, where he died a few years ago; Edward Ault, now in Morrisburg, whose son, Charles, thirty years later, was one of Mr. Whitney's most promising pupils, and who is now an artist of repute in the city of Cleveland; Orson Soules, for many years a telegraph operator, now a farmer in the Township of Matilda; Charles Ault, a brother of Edward, who died young; William Johnston, the son of a widowed mother, one of the brightest boys in the school. He became a printer, published the *Iroquois Chief* during the Brouse-Crawford election in 1858, and for some time thereafter; later the *Cornwall Economist* and *Port Hope Guide;* and then became, next to Gordon Brown, the leading editor of the Toronto *Globe*, but died before he reached his fortieth year.

Robert Harkness, eldest brother of the present Chairman, appeared to acquire knowledge without an effort, and valued it about in proportion to the effort when acquired. He did business awhile as a general merchant at Dixon's Corners, and later in Iroquois, in what is now the Powell House. He was two years Clerk of the Township and one year in the Village Council. In 1862 he went to British Columbia, travelling with a party overland from Winnipeg, taking their supplies on the backs of oxen, that had to be killed and eaten when the party reached the mountains. Being the only one of the adventurers who knew anything about lumbering, he superintended the construction of a raft on the head waters of the Fraser River, and navigated it down the unknown rapids with the supplies, while his companions made their way past the dangerous places by land. A few years later he returned; taught school for a short time, visited friends in Ireland, was again Township Clerk, kept hotel, became a Justice of the Peace, and finally closed his career as editor of the Picton *Times*, just as he had passed his fiftieth year.

Jacob Lowery, a quiet and thoughtful student, was the eldest of a family of seven, all of whom early fell victims to consumption. A stone in Point Iroquois Cemetery, with the simple inscription, "The Lowery Family," marks the resting-place of the father, mother, and seven children—three sons and four daughters.

David A. Breakenridge, a medical student, was the exquisite of the school. Just before the commencement of one of the terms, bills were posted announcing the opening and giving the names of the several members of the staff. "Jake" Lowery, who had a keen sense of humor, and detested anything like foppery, sketched a recognizable caricature of Breakenridge on one of these bills, and wrote under it, "*Dr. Puff, Professor of Etiquette.*" The epithet had an appropriateness that commended it to the boys, and poor Breakenridge never got altogether over it while he remained in Iroquois. He soon after abandoned medicine, except as a druggist, and later became a very successful life insurance agent. About 1893 he died in Brockville.

H. H. Cook, a young man from the Township of Williamsburg, also attended the school about this time. He afterwards

T. G. WILLIAMS, D.D.
ARTHUR BROWN, I.P.S.   H. H. ROSS, M.A., M.P.
A. W. MORRISON.
W. S. JOHNSTON.   A. S. ROSE, I.P.S.

engaged with his brother in lumbering, and is now among the wealthy men of the country: has been several years in the Local Legislature and in Parliament, and, though not there now, is still on the right side of sixty, and may again be heard from.

Robert, or "Bob" Larmour also belonged to this period. He turned his attention to telegraphing, became Superintendent of a Division on the Grand Trunk Railway, and subsequently Managing Director of the London and Port Stanley Railway. He is still living.

Thomas G. Williams was the son of that William H. Williams who conducted the great revival camp-meeting on the "Point" in 1823. He was born near Belleville about 1836 or 1837. His mother was the sister of Charles C. Rose, whom we have also mentioned in connection with the founding of the school. The home of her people was at Dixon's Corners, and when the elder Williams retired from the active ministry he settled there. "Tom" entered the Grammar School here in the fall of 1856, when Mr. Carman was principal, and continued in it, teaching betimes, through Cowan's time and the first year or two of Mr. Whitney's. Subsequently he attended Victoria College. In 1861 he entered on probation for the ministry, and was ordained in 1865. His progress towards a front place in the Church was thereafter steady, if not very rapid. He was stationed at the following places: Rawdon, Huntingdon, Franklin Centre, Winchester, Iroquois, Prescott, Brockville, Pembroke; Sherbrooke Street, Montreal; West End, Montreal; and is now in Sherbrooke City; was Chairman of District fifteen years, and twice President of the Montreal Conference; a member of the General Conference in 1878, and of each General Conference since; a member of the General Board of Missions since 1883, and Secretary for eleven years. But the work for which he should be longest and most gratefully remembered was the union of the Methodist Churches in Canada. The union of the Presbyterian Churches in 1875, had directed public attention to the question of the union of the two branches of the Methodist

Church, and the matter had been pretty freely talked over here during Mr. Williams' incumbency, from 1876 to 1879; but no action was taken until the fall of 1881, when Mr. Williams, who was then stationed in Prescott, and was Chairman of the Brockville District, summoned several of his leading ministers to meet with ministers of the Methodist Episcopal Church at Morrisburg, on December 15th.

This was the first meeting held to promote union. Mr. Williams presided, and the outcome was a call to all the official members of the Methodist Church of Canada in the Brockville District, and of the Ottawa District of the Methodist Episcopal Church, to meet at Iroquois, on the 1st of February, 1882. Mr. Williams was again chosen to preside. Over six hundred were in attendance, and the Union movement was got fairly under way. A paper, called the *Methodist Union*, was started, and published at the office of the *Morrisburg Herald*, Mr. Williams contributing liberally to its columns until the Churches were finally united. Bishop Carman was then the head of the Methodist Episcopal Church, and was at first regarded as being unfriendly, but he subsequently led the movement from the other side; and to these two men, more than to any others, it is due that we now have but one Methodist Church in Canada.

Mr. (now Dr.) Williams has written several pamphlets, mostly controversial, and one book, "Methodism and Anglicanism in the Light of Scripture and History." This is now included in the curriculum of students reading for the degree of Bachelor of Divinity in the Wesleyan Theological College, Montreal. The Doctor has fought many hard battles in behalf of the Scott Act, and believes that a prohibitive Act might be enforced as effectually as any of our Customs regulations. In addition to the positions named, he has been a member of the Board of Examiners of Probationers since 1874, and is a member of the Board of Governors of the Wesleyan Theological College, Montreal. He was also President of the Ministerial Association in Montreal in 1894, composed of ministers of all Protestant Churches in the city.

William H. Williams, a younger brother, was also a student, and finished his school course here. He was for many years a writer on the Toronto *Globe*; first, as correspondent during the first Riel troubles, and later as sporting editor. He is now in New Orleans, still, we believe, doing newspaper work.

Alexander Morrison was born in the Township of Mountain, in 1846. His father, James Morrison, is of Scotch descent, but came to this country from Ireland, where the family had been domiciled long enough to make of him a pretty good Irishman. He is impetuous in manner, outspoken, enterprising, hospitable, and generous—characteristics, some at least of which have descended to his son. His enterprise brought him a fair measure of success, and in 1856 he purchased a fine farm and residence on the St. Lawrence, near the western boundary of Matilda, where he still lives, bearing jauntily the weight of eighty-two years. Alexander attended the Public School at the neighboring village of Cardinal until sufficiently advanced, when he entered the Iroquois Grammar School, and spent three or four years under Mr. Whitney. He then decided on a mercantile course, and went to the British American Commercial College, Toronto, from which, in due course, he received a diploma. With this as his principal capital, he determined to tempt fortune in the Golden State, and in the winter of 1868 sailed from New York for San Francisco. There he soon got a good clerical position in one of the leading hotels, the "American Exchange." Ten months thereafter he came home on a visit, intending to return to the "American Exchange;" but, just as he was leaving a second time, a lady in Iroquois asked him to stop at Sacramento and see her son, who was in that city. This he promised to do, little thinking that it would result in changing his plans and affect his whole future life. He reached Sacramento on Saturday, and saw his friend. On Monday he accepted a position as clerk in the "Western Hotel," of which he is still the manager. His life has since been uneventful; his surplus earnings have been well invested, and he is in easy circumstances. He has been very generous to his less fortunate friends, and still retains his love for his old home and his *alma mater*.

Hugo H. Ross is the eldest son of the late John S. Ross, and was born in Iroquois in 1847. He must have entered the Grammar School when under ten years of age, as he was a pupil of Dr. Carman's. He remained in the school through Cowan's, Davies', and the first three or four years of Mr. Whitney's time, when he entered Toronto University, graduating about 1869, and taking the Silver Medal. He then devoted himself to High School work for a time, but his father's business was large and required more attention than he could spare from his parliamentary duties, and the young man was called home to assist in its management. Subsequently a partnership was formed, consisting of the father and two sons, H. H. and Allan J., and known as Ross. Bros. & Co., dealers in hardware, grain, etc. The business has been continued by the sons since the father's death. "Hugo" was always a favorite in social circles in Iroquois, and succeeded to a large share of his father's popularity in the county. In 1891 he was elected to Parliament, though by a narrow majority, but his native village, for the first time in its history, placed a Conservative at the head of the poll.

Among his contemporaries, Robert Baldwin Carman, the second son of Philip Carman, is one of the best known. He was born in 1843, educated here and at Albert College, where he took his degree of B.A. in 1866. He then took a course in Chemistry, Zoology, and Botany at the St. Lawrence Scientific School, in connection with Harvard University, Boston; was Professor of Chemistry at Albert University some years, but finally turned his attention to law, and became a barrister in 1873. He soon after entered into partnership with James Leitch, of Cornwall. In 1883 he became Junior County Judge of these Counties, a position he still holds.

Another, Andrew Harkness, a brother of the present Chairman of the High School Board, entered the school about 1863, when eighteen years of age. He was at the time an untamed youth, and severely tested Mr. Whitney's confessedly superior skill as a disciplinarian; but he eventually proved himself a good student, studied Medicine at McGill College, Montreal, taking the primary prize in 1868, and the final prize in 1869, when he graduated. He is now practising at Lancaster.

Not many of the "old boys" of the school were boys so long or, when they became men, were so much in sympathy with the younger boys as William Henry Patton. He was the son of Arthur Patton, Esq., of this village, and, on his mother's side, the grandson of James Armstrong, a wealthy and influential resident of Ogdensburg, N.Y. When but a boy of sixteen, or thereabouts, he was, through the influence of his grandfather's family, appointed American Vice-Consul at Prescott. Later, he got a place in the establishment of A. T. Stewart, New York. While there he became New York correspondent of some Canadian papers, and on his return was for a time a reporter for the *Montreal Star*. The last ten years of his life he devoted to keeping his father's books, and sounding the praises of his native village through the local papers of surrounding towns. His local patriotism was unbounded, and he was at once the promoter and chronicler of the sports and pastimes of the people, as well as of every movement tending to progress or improvement. He died in 1890.

John Earl Halliwell entered the school about 1869. He was the son of the Rev. John Halliwell, who created a sensation here a quarter of a century ago by leaving the Methodist Episcopal Church and uniting with the Church of England. The young man subsequently graduated, and studied law. He also joined the volunteers, and served as Lieutenant under Colonel Williams during the North-West Rebellion. At Batoche he received a gun-shot wound in the shoulder, and is still disabled. He is now practising law at Stirling.

There are others of the boys of the sixties whose lives we would like to trace, but the field widens as we proceed, and we have already exceeded our limit of space. Besides, Mr. Whitney has gone over this ground in his paper, and we would only be enlarging on what he has said.

Alexander S. Rose belongs to a later period. He was born at Dixon's Corners sometime near 1860. His father, Alva Rose, was a nephew of the Charles C. Rose who was among the first promoters of the Grammar School, and was a man of much more than average intelligence. He was, however, not successful in business, and young Rose had to make his own way in the world. After leaving the Public School he and his brother engaged in brickmaking at South Mountain. This does not appear to have been congenial work for either, as it was soon abandoned, and Alexander entered the High School. After becoming qualified to teach, he went to Manitoba, and has since devoted himself to school work. He is now regarded as being among the best educationists in that province, and is Inspector of Public Schools for the Brandon District, or Division.

At school with Mr. Rose were two boys, both cousins of his, who have reflected credit on the school, and whom Mr. Whitney has failed to notice: Arthur Whitney, his eldest son, who graduated in Medicine at Queen's College, Kingston—standing very close to the Gold Medal—and who is now a successful practitioner in St. Paul; and Fred. B. Harkness, second son of the Robert Harkness who was among Mr. Dick's pupils, and who, while attending lectures in the same College, maintained himself by working part of each day at his trade of printer, and yet won the Gold Medal at graduation. He is now practising medicine at North Gower.

VILLAGE VIEWS.

CHAPTER XV.

The Reunion.

URING the latter part of 1894 some of the old students, notably Mr. John S. Carstairs and Mrs. Wm. M. Doran—the Mary Elliot whom Mr. Whitney speaks of as being one of two pupils whom he found in the school one morning during the fever plague of 1867—began to talk of, in some way, marking the semi-centennial of the High School. Soon after a few of the old-time pupils and friends of the school got together and decided to celebrate the event by a reunion of the "old boys" and "girls," and, if the necessary funds could be obtained, the publication of a memorial volume. It then appeared that Mr. Jackson, the Principal, had also contemplated some kind of celebration, and it was thought best to call a larger meeting. This meeting was held in the early part of 1895, and it was found that considerable difference of opinion existed as to what should be done, or attempted, and a committee was appointed to deal with the matter. This committee consisted of Mr. Whitney, James Bullis, Mr. Jackson (the Principal), Mr. E. McNulty (the Secretary of the High School Board), John G. Harkness, B.A., and Arthur Forward, B.A. (old students), and Adam Harkness, in whose office the meetings were held. After considering the various schemes proposed, it was finally agreed that the original plan should be carried out, and sub-committees were appointed. To John G. Harkness, James Bullis and Mr. E. McNulty was left the care of the finances, and to Messrs. Jackson, Whitney and Adam Harkness was entrusted the

preparation of the memorial volume, or history of the school. The writing of this subsequently devolved entirely on the last named, while Mr. Jackson attended to the illustrations and assisted the members of the Finance Committee.

Monday, the 2nd of September, Labor Day, was selected as the time for the reunion or celebration. The speakers were chosen with special reference to their relations to the school and their familiarity with its history. On the Friday following a report of the meeting was published in the *St. Lawrence News*. It tells its own story, and we give it as it appeared, except the synopsis of the speeches and papers of Dr. Carman, Mr. Whitney, James A. Carman, Mr. Carstairs and Dr. Harkness, which we have published in full in the Appendix.

JUBILEE OF THE HIGH SCHOOL.

A DAY TO BE REMEMBERED A HALF CENTURY HENCE.

Fitting Celebration of a Notable Anniversary—Speeches and Speeches— Funds for the Memorial Volume all Subscribed.

There could not be a finer day for the occasion once in fifty years than was Monday, when the Semi-Centennial of the Iroquois High School was duly celebrated according to the announced programme. The sun was warm, but the atmosphere had a bracing autumnal touch that made its warmth welcome, and there was no wind, nor dust, nor shadflies, nor aught else to make a half-day in the open air otherwise than perfectly agreeable.

There were a great many speeches throughout the day and evening. The criticism of the younger element was that, taking them "by and large," there were too many, and it might have been an improvement had some of them been curtailed, or had there been fewer speakers. But the speeches were all able and vital to the occasion, and from first to last were listened to with keen appreciation by large numbers of the foremost and most intelligent men and women of the community. It was interesting, and to the dispassionate listener, somewhat amusing, to see the perennial and ubiquitous question of religious teaching in the schools cropping out again and again, and to hear the hopelessly diverging views of the different speakers.

Taking it as a whole the celebration was very fitting, very creditable and enjoyable, and reflects honor on those who carried it out in the face of considerable apathy and discouragement at the beginning.

SEMI-CENTENNIAL OF IROQUOIS HIGH SCHOOL. 129

Perhaps it is not out of place here to give a special word of praise to Mr. Jackson and Mr. J. G. Harkness, by whose efforts mainly the funds for the memorial volume were obtained. The probable worth of this work is perhaps scarcely recognized. To say nothing of its present value and interest, it should be a monument more enduring than marble. It is not hard to imagine how a copy of this work will be prized when the Centennial of the School is celebrated.

At the announced time, 2.30 p.m., about seven hundred of old and young of both sexes, a large preponderance being ex-pupils, assembled on the High School grounds, where seats had been laid and a platform was erected.

There were seated on the platform besides the speakers, Rev. R. L. M. Houston, Rev. J. M. Macalister, Rev. F. G. Lett, Dr. Williams of Cardinal, Messrs. J. N. Tuttle, N. G. Sherman and Robert Bouck.

After a few remarks by the Chairman, Dr. Harkness, Mr. J. A. Jackson, B.A., the present headmaster of the school, delivered a brief and appropriate address of welcome. He stated that the full amount of $400 for the memorial volume had been subscribed, and it was assured that the volume would be published at an early date. He read letters of regret from a number of teachers and officials of neighboring schools, and a very interesting letter from James A. Carman, B.A., Mr. Jackson's predecessor in the headmaster's chair. . . .

Mr. J. S. Carstairs gave an address of considerable length, dealing with his connection with the school as student and teacher, and having also many well-expressed thoughts on education in general. . . .

H. H. Ross, M.A., M.P., spoke briefly and humorously. He alluded to one time when, as a small boy, he was under Dr. Carman's tutelage, and played truant to go in swimming. Dr. Carman's eagle eye detected the malfeasance, and the speaker was taken captive and locked in a closet, and left to his own reflection for some time; and after this the Doctor further chastened him by applying the rod, with a hand that was not heavy, however. Under Mr. Whitney he had spent many pleasant hours, and he always found him a friend in and out of school. He also spoke of the brief *régime* of Mr. Davies. Referring to Mr. Carstairs' allusion to the matter of religious teaching in the school, Mr. Ross intimated that he was then on delicate ground. For the past twelve months he and his colleagues in Parliament had been making a study of this question as it affected another province, and they had found out one thing about it, that it was not a safe matter to talk about. There was room for argument on both sides, but he himself would not argue the question, for the audience might then learn how he was going to vote in Parliament. In concluding, Mr. Ross spoke in terms of praise of the present status and prospects of the school, and mentioned that in passing through Mountain and Winchester lately he found the school had high repute in those townships. A straw showing how the wind blows was the fact that Mr. Kennedy, who lives on the line between Mountain and Winchester, had told him he was going to send a couple of boys to the Iroquois school by preference to others equally or more convenient, for the reason that he believed this to be the best school.

Mr. W. A. Whitney, M.A., followed with a paper reviewing the history of the school during the long term that he was headmaster. This paper, coming from the man who, of all men, has had most to do with the school, could not fail to be of exceptional interest.

Dr. Carman was next called upon, and was given quite an ovation. The Rev. Doctor spoke with a force, earnestness and clearness which showed that advancing years have not deprived him of his remarkable physical and mental vigor. . . .

THE EVENING MEETING.

In the evening the Town Hall was literally packed. Not only all the regular seats, but chairs and benches in the aisles, and even the steps leading to the green-room doors, were occupied. In the absence of Mr. C. E. Cameron, Reeve, whose letter of regret was read by Mr. Jackson, Mr. N. G. Sherman occupied the chair, and after a few remarks, in which he contrasted the schools of his childhood with those of to-day, called on Rev. J. M. Macalister.

Mr. Macalister said that this celebration was one of the most important events in the history of the village. The school to a greater or less extent must have its influence on every person in the village. He felt that all honor was due to the large-hearted, noble-minded men who founded the school. He also eulogized the school and staff of to-day; and, in conclusion, said he had a suggestion to make. Of all who attend the High School, the great mass finish their scholastic education within its walls and for the benefit of these and others the village needed a third educational institution, viz., a library. The opportunity offered now to have a free public library in Iroquois, and it was his hope that the institution would be established.

Rev. F. G. Lett began by saying that his mind reverted to the year 1862, when he and others of his family blazed a road through the woods to get to a log schoolhouse. In that schoolhouse he learned to think. The man who was teaching knew how to make a boy think for himself. As one of the religious leaders of the community he was in full sympathy with the promoters of the High School. Their objects were the same. He mentioned that he would like to see the school have a gymnasium, and predicted that the next half-century would see far greater progress than the past.

Rev. Father Twomey made a brief and scholarly address, speaking eloquently of the influence of education in taking away the mind from things that degrade it. He believed that the Iroquois High School was governed by a grand Board, and would continue to prosper. Regarding the matter of religious instruction in the schools, on which other speakers had been free to express themselves, he would refrain from giving his views ; he believed that it would be improper, not to say impertinent, to speak on this occasion, when all should be harmony, on a subject on which there were such radically and irreconcilably divergent views.

Dr. Harkness, before reading his paper, recalled the days when he was a student at the High School. As student and trustee he had been so long connected with the school that it had become part of his existence. . . .

Miss Libbie Beach was now called upon to sing, and had a warm reception. She rendered a very difficult selection, "The Echo Song," by Eckert, in an accomplished manner, and for encore gave a sweet and expressive rendition of "Home, Sweet Home." On her recall Miss Beach was presented with a beautiful bouquet, the gift of the High School.

Rev. R. L. M. Houston presented the regrets of Rev. T. J. Stiles, who was so occupied with parish work that he could not be present. He was glad to return to Iroquois and see familiar faces and shake friendly hands. It was a great thing to have the youth educated. The best evidence he could offer of his opinion of the Iroquois High School was that he was thinking of sending his daughter to the school. Education was the training of the mind so the mind would think for itself. The most educated man, the wisest man, is the man who feels he knows scarcely anything. There is no end to knowledge ; education is never complete, it will never be complete until we cease to see through a glass darkly. The speaker had an opinion with which he knew many would disagree, but he had no hesitation in expressing it—that there was one lack in the school system, a lack that the country feels. We have the three R's, Reading, 'Riting and 'Rithmetic ; there is a fourth R, a far more important R, that was lacking and should and must be supplied, namely, Religion. He believed that morals and religion could not be divorced.

Mr. Arthur Brown, I.P.S., touched upon the time when he was a student here, in 1851-2, and read from an old journal an account of the offering of prizes to teachers and trustees for good school work, by John A. Carman, George Brouse and William Elliot. He believed that in the selection of teachers too great attention was paid to their accomplishments, and too little sometimes to their character.

Mr. Jamieson, Principal of the Morrisburg Collegiate Institute, began by paying a graceful compliment to Miss Beach, saying that

Iroquois might well be proud of her sweet singer, a sentiment that was heartily applauded. He also complimented the teachers of Iroquois, and said that the rivalry between the two High Schools of Dundas was a friendly rivalry ; each school was the better for there being two.

Dr. Carman was then finally called upon, and after speaking feelingly of the inexpressible pleasure it gave him to return to his native village and rejoice with its people in the advancement of education, he reverted to the question of religious teaching in the schools. If the State is to put religion in the schools, he asked, what religion will the State put there ? He again expressed himself as uncompromisingly opposed to any attempt to introduce religious teaching in the schools.

The meeting closed with the singing of " God Save the Queen."

APPENDIX.

Introductory—Dr. Carman—W. A. Whitney—James A. Carman—
J. S. Carstairs—Dr. Harkness.

NDER our present system of education the whole cost of the Primary or Public schools, five-sixths of that of the High schools, and a considerable proportion of that of the Colleges, Technical Schools and Universities, is provided for by general taxation, and in the Public schools the attendance is compulsory. The State prescribes the studies, and directs the conduct of the school in every particular. It appears to have become accepted as an axiomatic truth, that it is one of the first duties of the Government to see that every child born in the country is properly fitted for the duties of citizenship, and thus the whole population of school age may be said to be wards of the State.

This condition has come upon us gradually, almost imperceptibly. When our fathers gathered at the cross-roads and built their little log school-houses, so that they might by mutual co-operation save their children from growing up altogether unlettered, it never occurred to them that they were not individually responsible ; that it was not a part of the duty of a parent to provide mental as well as physical sustenance for his children. But even then the seed was planted that has grown into the gigantic tree, in the shadow of which we are now resting.

The small grants that were being made by the Government were primarily intended to encourage local effort, and were based to some extent on results. This led to Governmental supervision, at first slight, but gradually increasing, until now the people, through their Local Boards of Trustees, have very little to say in the management of their schools, their duties and powers being almost exclusively confined to providing a certain specified accommodation for the children of school age within their respective sections, and selecting and employing teachers whose qualifications have been approved by the central authority. The books, the mode of teaching, everything connected with the imparting of instruction within the school, is uniform and under the direct control and supervision of the Government. The whole of the youth of the country are being run in one mould, the goal being that we may rear a race intelligent, patriotic and united.

The main obstacles in the way of this are the fear of the influence of the secular school on the future religious life of the pupil, and the desire of the French-speaking people to preserve the literature, language and traditions of their race. The first leads the dominating Protestant churches, though in favor of a national system of education, to endeavor to engraft on the ordinary work of the school a certain amount of religious teaching and practice, while the two combined have been the cause of the demand made on behalf of the French and Catholics that they be allowed to control the education of their own children in schools separate from those of the rest of the community. This right, with certain limitations, was conceded in Ontario before Confederation, and at the time of the Union was made a part of the pact. Since then it has been extended somewhat, but the extension has been accompanied by increased supervision on the part of the State. Similar rights were conceded in Manitoba, but were withdrawn in 1890, and the minority is now appealing to the Dominion Government for their restoration, thus bringing the question before the whole country, and making the imparting of religious instruction in the schools a subject of absorbing interest to all connected with our educational institutions. It was freely dealt with by the speakers at the "Reunion," and three of the papers that follow may be said to represent three important phases of thought on the question.

The Rev. Dr. Carman, the head and representative of a youthful and aggressive ecclesiastical organization, though profoundly imbued with the realities of the spiritual life and the need of religious instruction, is yet prepared to leave all that to the Church, the Sunday School and the home, that all the rising generation may gather in the Public school, as their fathers gather at the market-place or the town meeting. We cannot but admire his broad Catholicity, his earnestness and his abounding faith in the cause of the Master whom he so zealously serves.

The views of Mr. Carstairs appear to accord pretty fully with those of what may be called the historic churches—churches that have ceased to be aggressive, and are more careful to retain their own adherents than eager to enter into conflict for new recruits. They appear to have grasped the fact so plainly written on every page of the world's history, that we are very largely the creatures of environment, and, in nine cases out of ten, hold our religious opinions because they were implanted in us when we were young.

Dr. Harkness, with much less faith in religious impressions as a base on which to rear the moral edifice, recognizes, perhaps, even more fully the plastic nature of the material with which the schoolmaster has to deal, and the necessity of cultivating the moral as well as the intellectual side of our nature. He would teach, not only what right living is, but that every deviation from it brings with unerring certainty its corresponding punishment. Without sacrificing moral training in the school, he would find common ground for all classes and creeds in a system of scientific ethics, about the correctness of which there could be no dispute.

ADDRESSES DELIVERED AT THE SEMI-CENTENNIAL CELEBRATION OF THE IROQUOIS HIGH SCHOOL.

BY REV. DR. CARMAN.

The celebration of a jubilee is the celebration of efforts, deliverances and achievements; the commemoration of men, and their enterprises and deeds. It is also the forecast of plans, purposes and hopes. Standing upon the high ground of the present, it turns its piercing, gleaming eye upon the past and the future. God appointed to His ancient people these seasons for religious and patriotic ends, that they might well consider their ways, wisely order their paths, and stand mighty and glorious amid the nations. Such a celebration looks two ways: contemplating the foundations laid and the structures to be reared; reckoning the mile stones passed and the distance yet to be travelled. It records facts, and makes promises and covenants; it stereotypes history, and justifies and illuminates prophecy. It raises the questions: What has been done? How was it done? What remains to be done? How shall we do it? It starts the inquiries: Was the object in view a good one? Have the efforts to accomplish it paid? Where were the failures? Where the successes? Can we avoid the failures in the future? Can we multiply and enlarge the successes? Who are the men and the women that went before us? What heritage did they leave? How are we, with our greater opportunities, discharging our trust and meeting the claims upon us? What kind of a heritage shall we leave to those who come after us?

The only way we can pay our debt to our ancestors—to the founders of our nation and the builders of our institutions—is to guard and enrich those about us, to found and build for posterity. "What has posterity done for me?" is the reply of the trickster and the low politician; it is base ingratitude and treason against mankind. What our predecessors did for our generation they did for the human race; and in the name of the human race, and by its energy and imperial claim, they laid us under the weightiest obligations to all the generations to come. So our debt is to the human race, and we can pay our debt to the human race only by paying it loyally and liberally to posterity, and to the men of the fleeting present as we may catch the ever-escaping opportunity. The human race is the claimant, the unit of sovereignty and right. From it, under the government of God, we receive our benefits; and to it, under the same government, are due the highest consecration and best service of our heart and life. This is at once a noble Christianity and a generous civilization to devote us wholly to the good of our fellow-men; preserving the sacred memory of departed benefactors; and pouring richest treasures of religion, science and art into the laps of the oncoming procession of beneficiaries. And this is the high example of the Son of God, and the surest obedience to his supreme law of love. "No man liveth unto himself." As in the journeying of God's people out of the bondage of Egypt, the brightness beckoned onward, and the shades were thrown upon the way they had travelled; so, in the generations of the human race and the progress of humanity, mixed evil and good are left behind in colors sober and subdued, while aspiration and hope lighten up the whole sky in the direction of our advance.

Fifty years have gone since the opening of this Educational Institution. The school itself has seen its changes; it has passed through various phases, from the voluntary Academy at its origin on the basis of self-support, to the Governmental High School as it is now in vital connexion with our public and provincial system. The very building erected by its founder has given place to the present noble edifice, more in harmony, it may be, with modern requirements and appointments. The plain two-storey blue limestone structure of half a century ago, whose walls were quarried from the bed of the neighboring canal, and in their solidity stood fit emblem of the education desired by the men that built it, is supplanted by an airier fabric and a lighter architecture. Amid these scenes the fitting question of the hour forces itself upon us: The fathers, where are they? Where is John Adam Carman, whose was the conception, the plan and the execution of the project? Where are James Coons and Matthew Coons, the two brothers who jointly gave the land on which the building stands? Where are Jacob Brouse, Philip Carman and John S. Ross, who were charter Trustees, and faithful friends and supporters of the enterprise? Not one of them survives to share in the gladness of this celebration, and most of them finished their earthly career many years ago. And where are the heads of the large families of Shavers, Aults, Dorans, Parlows, Tuttles, Services, Wallaces, Brouses, Coonses and Carmans, that formed a large part of the patronizing constituency at the time of the opening of the school? Gone to the land unknown, most of them, with their contemporaries long ago; and their grandchildren and great-grandchildren are now the scholars in the seats and on the play-ground. What a commentary on the instability of human affairs! What an evidence that the things that are seen are temporal, while the things that are unseen are enduring and eternal. The same science, the same truth, but teachers and scholars all changed! What a call upon us all to set uprightness of character on high, and build well into Church and State and common humanity; for we ourselves must soon disappear. All there will be of us will be what we have done for God and country, and for the human race.

Standing upon this Lookout Mountain, the vantage ground of this Semi-Centennial commemoration, this place of review and prospect, I am reminded of the school-boy's horizon, the circuit that bounded my view in the earlier years, and swept onward and outward into the wider circles of subsequent life. I well remember when the glowing sky met the fruitful earth up at Gordon Wert's and Samuel Shaver's, the western limit of School Section No. 4. There was a haze beyond even to the Edwardsburg village; but the houses from which the lads and lassies came to our school were on the utmost verge of well-defined habitation. The sun set at Samuel Shaver's, and rose somewhere about Flagg's Bridge, while there was an eastern gloaming over Mariatown, and even a little beyond. In the north was an auroral play about Dixon's Corners, especially at election time, when the spirits were free; and in the south an austral brilliancy about Waddington and Ogdensburg, the limits of milling and trading expeditions. This vast expanse of the world of boyhood comprised some four or five school sections, and it was the school section that was the constituent unit, the province of childhood's Dominion, everything pivoted upon the "little brown schoolhouse," the centre of interest and the source of power. There were the boys that contended in the game; and there the girls that made our hearts flutter, we knew not how or why. In those days there were no Separate schools, and all people of all classes learned of one grammar, one arithmetic and one history, in the interests of one Empire, and of the common brotherhood of man. Would it were so to-day. Within this spacious territory was everything found necessary to the tastes, and sports and dreams of opening youth. Here were the preachers and parsons; I have them yet in my mind and heart. Here were the schoolmasters—schoolmistresses, an invention of recent times, were then scarce—but the schoolmasters, those sages of antiquity, those sublime mortals of dignity and importance, those oracles of wisdom and grand viziers in pomp and authority, that walked amid our puerilities like Mars among pigmies—Jupiter tonans! How we trembled in their presence and fled from their frown! how we hung upon their lips to announce the recess, or a half holiday, or the dismissal of school! How we feared they might keep us after school, and away on till dark! And that rule! when it would come along, straightening up our toes and our backbones! Not much curvature of the spine in those days. Those were not the days when little boys and girls, doctored up by a Minister of

Education and his Normal and Model schools, taught the youth of the land. How well I remember some of those giants of antiquity, the predecessors of the "beardless" girls and bicycling boys that now do the pedagoguing. For instance, there was John J. Kerr, a retired soldier, a stalwart Irishman, and a polished "English" gentleman. He was the man that used to say to the Trustees, he would put the soldiers—us boys—through their facing till the army was disbanded. He meant he'd keep us straight till school was out. What a pretty, soft, well formed hand he had, and how proud he was of it. How beautifully he could write. He lifted the standard for good writing in all these parts. And he had Lennie and Walkingame at his finger ends. Then there was an American gentleman, Samuel Platt, Esq. He was grand on school exhibitions, and could bring down the house every time with his "Night Before Christmas." And there was John F. Ault, of School Section No. 2, a Canadian born and bred, a connecting link and sort of John the Baptist of the new dispensation. He was the man that could make figures plain, and bring the scholar easily through the mazes of Double Rule of "Three" and "Tare" and "Tret." What a bound was there onward when Hiram F. Gates, a well worn student, and his faculty opened classes in the Seminary, the foundation whose superstructure we to-day magnify and admire. His face was calm, his motions slow, his judgments swift, his comprehension of his work clear, and his devotion to it ardent. I see him now, looking through those glasses, and, with the grace and ease of a sovereign, moving about the class-room. His successor, Alexander Dick, was a brusque, decided man, who told you with his lips, without speaking, when his mind was made up. Mr. Gates was a Presbyterian, and Mr. Dick a Baptist, which showed the genuine Catholicity of the benefactor of the people who laid these foundations. Time would fail to trace the bright succession down to a Whitney, a James Carman, and a Jackson, the reigning sovereign. They left their traces, and did their work. Their record is in our unfolding history.

Ours is the present obligation and opportunity. It is ours to build upon the foundations already laid. If, perchance, they have been laid in poor material, or daubed with untempered mortar, it is ours to remove them, and to do better work. We may find no fault with the past, but avoid as best we can defects and mistakes in the future. In our country's interest and the interest of mankind we must build intelligence into the grand fabric, and morality and religion. We must build in patriotism, loyalty, and honest government. We must build in industry, economy and thrift. We must secure a free Church in a free State. We must strengthen the school, the bank and the mart. We must guard the purity of the home, the honesty of the government, and the justice of the court. We must jealously protect the freedom of the press, the freedom of conscience, and the freedom of worship. Every age brings its conflicts, and every generation has its sacred trusts. Even now in Manitoba and the North-West is our school system in danger. A previous speaker has rather implied that Manitoba should be coerced into the adoption of Ultramontane schools. Likely the best thing, in all the circumstances, for our Dominion Government to do is to let Manitoba manage her own educational affairs.

Having so precious a heritage to guard we can well see what it is our duty to avoid. We must shun the systems that nurture ignorance, sectionalism, or sectarianism in our schools. We must shun violent partisanship and dishonest government. We must shun immorality and irreligion, and the vices that at once nourish them and fatten on them. A time-serving press or pulpit should be an abomination to our people. If we are to build up a rugged national character, we must put far away from us and keep away every influence that will weaken the marriage tie or corrupt the home. The moral bond, the fear of God, the love of man, the strength of conscience and the sanctions of religion must be maintained in their integrity. What other thought or aspiration founded this institution of learning? What was then in the mind of John A. Carman but the conviction that knowledge and religion must be conjoined in the personal and national character? Indeed, what with him, and with those that were with him in this work, was the prime motive of action but love of man and faith in Jesus Christ the Saviour of men, as the best evidence and expression of that love? Whether it be Christian education or an educated Christianity, those men thoroughly believed in it. We may not banish or exclude ourselves into separate schools for sectarian purposes, but we must give to our education the glow of Christianity, and to our Christianity the wealth of a sound education. The God above us has given us a goodly land, an honorable ancestry, and a fortunate and blessed national inheritance. For the most part descended from the United Empire Loyalists, we may well be grateful for our relationship to the British Empire so glorious in history and so mighty for good among the nations to-day.

Love of British Institutions, of the British Sovereignty, Crown and Flag, was the ruling impulse, the guiding star of the men and women that settled this Upper Canadian St. Lawrence valley. They were United Empire Loyalists. They proved their faith in Britain, their devotion to the Crown, by toils, privation, heroism and sacrifice of an unexampled character. Britain's measures may have been, in some respects, arbitrary and unjustifiable; her treatment of the colonists, unworthy of the Motherland; and the revolt of those who stood out upon principle against her exactions to their heart and conscience a sacred duty; and, certainly, the event might seem to cast no doubts or reflections on the justice of their cause. In the Providence of God the British flag went down at

Boston and New York, and in the same good providence it arose in strength and splendor over Quebec and Montreal. We are not to contemplate these great changes in human national affairs outside the divine government of men. If they were right who revolted and flew to arms, they certainly were right who believed that all grievances could be redressed by constitutional and parliamentary means, and therefore refused to enter the lists of war against the Mother Country. And again the event has justified their affection for their kinsmen and their fidelity to the Crown. The United Empire Loyalists settled in a vast wilderness, but a wilderness of immense capabilities. Under their hand, with God's blessing, it soon blossomed as the rose. What homes they planted! What communities they formed! What institutions they founded and reared! Though they would not revolt they were not renegades or slaves. They proved their love of liberty, piety and intelligence, their devotion to law and order by churches, schools, courts, councils and parliaments. They gave themselves to industry, and from fertile soil, flowing waters and teeming forests, wealth and comfort grew apace. God had given them a goodly land. Cities and towns respond to manufacture and art, and magnificent water and land highways to commerce and trade. Intelligence arose by education, and sense of duty by religious instruction. Scattered bands in the wilds became constituents of a great and growing people. And to-day surely we are not less inspired by the idea of a united Empire, not less attached to the noble institutions that have made our country what it is in our enjoyment this hour.

We have our plain duty: to build up this land in intelligence and freedom, in religion and sound knowledge.

By W. A. Whitney, M.A.

I have been asked by the Committee who have in charge this Semi-Centennial of the Iroquois High School to furnish a paper embracing some reminiscences of my connection with the school. In complying with this request, I find that I shall have to claim your indulgence for what may seem too free a use of the capital letter "I." I am compelled to rely almost wholly on my memory for what I may say, because, unfortunately, but few records have been preserved. At this half-way stage in the century, it is all-important that the scattered leaves of the school's history should be brought together, partly by what may be said to-day, and especially by the publication of the coming memorial volume. Those who may celebrate the Centennial of the institution fifty years hence will have ampler materials for such a memorial, as the Education Department now makes provision for keeping full records. In the last number of the *News* you will see that the second term of Dundas County Grammar School was opened on September 26th, 1846. Hence the school is now a little over forty-nine years old.

Out of the fifty years of the school's existence I was the Principal for nearly twenty-six consecutive years, so that I may claim, as did Æneas, "*Quorum magna pars fui*," which, being interpreted, means that I have had a large part in the history of the school. I believe that there is but one other man who has occupied one position as headmaster longer than I have. Almost my whole lifework has been given to this institution, and such abilities as I possessed have been devoted to the youth of this and adjacent counties. In April, 1860, Mr. Samuel Cowan, the Principal, asked me to take his place, as he was obliged to leave for Ireland. I lacked a few weeks of graduation, but the Board accepted me. The salary was $600, and I had no assistant. I found present about twenty-five pupils, and some of these were too young for High School work.

For several years after I became Principal there was no entrance examination. When the Education Department first exacted such a test, the High School Inspector had a sentence written on the blackboard, and the candidate was asked to parse the words. That was the only test, and that not very exacting. After this standard of entrance had been used for about three years, the Principal of each school was directed by Dr. Ryerson, the Chief Superintendent, to prepare examination papers on the usual studies of Common school work and, after examining the papers of the candidates, to pass or reject them.

My first Board of Trustees were: James Croil, Dr. Sherman, Alex. McDonald, Wm. Elliot, J. S. Ross and Philip Carman. Mr. Croil is the only one now living.

The Government grant was less than $400 per annum, and was given on the basis of the attendance of classical pupils. Neither the County Council nor the Village Council contributed a cent to the maintenance of the School. The pupils paid $8, $12 and $16 a year as fees, according to the subjects taken—Latin, Greek or French being the highest in price.

The school was called a seminary or academy at first, but when it became a part of the Provincial system, and for several years after I came—up to 1871—it was called the Matilda County Grammar School. The School year was divided into four terms of eleven weeks each. After I had been in the School a few months I told the Board that I was dissatisfied with the salary of $600, with the small attendance, and in having no assistant. They were somewhat shocked at my complaint, and said they saw no way of meeting my request. I then proposed that they should hand over to me the Government grant and fees, and I would employ a lady teacher as preceptress, and pay all charges for maintenance, insurance, etc. They readily and gladly agreed to the proposal. In October, 1860, I employed as preceptress, at $300 a year (a good salary for a lady at that time), Miss E. Bailey, of Potsdam.

There was an old piano in a small music-room on the second floor, which I got repaired and tuned, so that it was quite suitable for instruction and practice. Miss Bailey spent part of her time in giving lessons on the piano, and the rest in general teaching. Shortly after this new departure, I found that the number on the roll had increased from 25 to 70. We had pupils from all parts of the county—from Grenville and Stormont.

After meeting all demands, I still had over $700 per annum as my own salary.

There were no newspapers in the county in which to advertise, but we got out circulars, and even posters, and sent them far and wide.

This arrangement lasted for about six years, and the Board seemed well pleased and satisfied with my course. Finally, I became tired of collecting the fees at the end of each quarter, and asked the Board to relieve me of the burden and take the school into their own hands again. The Government grant had now increased greatly in consequence of the large attendance of classical pupils, and the income from fees now became quite respectable, so that the Board found themselves in possession of a surplus sufficient to make extensive changes and repairs on the building. It was originally designed for a boarding-school, with rooms for the principal and his family, and for a number of boarders, after the model of American academies. There were two class-rooms and a music-room. The living rooms were now no longer needed for their original purpose, and there was a need for larger class-rooms, because of the large attendance. The whole of the upper flat was thrown into one large school-room, to be occupied by the Principal and for assembly purposes.

The first grant to the school by the Village Council was $100 in 1865, for new seats for the Principal's class-room.

Another small amount was graciously given a little later on, but not until the law was changed in 1871 was the corporation obliged to contribute to the support of an institution that all considered their most valued possession, and that had very greatly contributed to the material, and especially the intellectual, advancement of the village and county. During the most of my time in the school I had a Board of Trustees who, by their harmonious action, their high standing and influence in the county, and their strong and increasing interest in behalf of the Grammar School, stood by me in my effort to maintain the attendance and general prosperity of the school.

Five years after I became the Principal we lost some pupils by the establishment of a Grammar School at Morrisburg. For several years thereafter we maintained the ascendancy, however, and not till that village had greatly surpassed Iroquois in wealth and population, and until the two townships to the north had much increased in wealth and educational enterprise, did the Morrisburg school, under the late Mr. Stuart, surpass us. In the year 1867, Iroquois was visited by a terrible scourge of typhoid fever. Very many of our homes lost one or more of their members, my first-born among the number. The effect on the school was, of course, disastrous. We kept our classes going, however, until barely two pupils—William Oxnam and Mary Elliot—answered to the roll-call. The Board then closed the doors for two months.

I look back with gratitude to the Giver of all good, that during those long twenty-six years I never was absent from my place through illness, except for a few days. I attribute this to the abundant physical exercise that I got from my long walk to and from school, and also to my flower and vegetable gardening, in which I have ever taken great delight.

The boys who love play more than study and restraint, no doubt were glad at my enforced absence one winter, from Monday morning till Thursday evening, when I became snowbound in Prescott, and there were no trains during all that time. My assistant, Miss Bailey, pluckily kept the school going, with the help of one of the senior pupils.

I had the following persons as my assistants, and in the following order: Miss E. Bailey (afterwards the wife of the late W. C. Bailey), Mrs. Whitney, Miss Weagant (of Morrisburg), Miss Stephens (of Cobourg—who married Rev. A. Bowerman and died in Winnipeg), Miss Holden (now Mrs. Chisholm, in California), Miss Anna Carman (now Mrs. W. L. Redmond), Miss Ada Lane, Mr. Ross, Mr. James A. Carman (who succeeded me as headmaster), my brother, Philo A. Whitney (now in Brantford), Mr. Clough, Mr. Lesslie (now a Church of England clergyman), Mr. Creelman (a lawyer in Toronto), Mr. Crosby (now headmaster at Forest), Mr. Alexander McLeod (a lawyer in Manitoba), Mr. Kinney, Mr. Montgomery (Mathematical-master in Petrolea), and Mr. Potter (who was my last assistant, and left when I did). You will wonder that the list is so large. The reason is that the Board thought they could not afford a salary sufficient to retain them. Some left to complete their education, or to receive higher salaries elsewhere. Most of them had no previous experience. The consequence was that I was sadly handicapped in my work of maintaining the efficiency of the school. Generally, I had to take all the advanced work in all the subjects of the course of study.

It was fortunate for me that at college I had taken a full pass course. When possible, I took all the Classics and English. After leaving Iroquois, I took and passed the examination for a specialist in Classics.

I exceedingly regret that the Educational Department made no regulation, as it does now, for keeping and preserving all the names of pupils, their studies and destiny. A very large number have passed through my hands. They are found in all the walks of life, and in places far distant.

The Church, the law, medicine, Parliament, the High and the Public school, commerce and the farm, have furnished places for their abilities and activities. I deem it a great honor that my teaching has helped to make those men and women useful to the world. Many have already finished life's work and have gone to an early reward. I can remember only two who died while at school—a son of Mr. Sydney Shaver, and a Miss Brockway. A few died before completing their college course, including Albert Coons, Donald McTavish, Simon Casselman, John Bennett and George Larmour. I have not room to give the names of all ex-pupils who have reflected honor on the old school, and it would seem invidious to particularize; still I cannot forbear to mention Dr. T. G. Williams, Dr. W. W. Carson, of Detroit; Albert VanCamp, of Cleveland; Mr. Guthrie, Mr. Service and Mr. Earle, in the Church. Clarke Moses is Public School Inspector of Haldimand, and A. S. Rose in Manitoba. Law is the chosen profession of James Ross, John Munro, Alexander McLeod, Albert Grier, John Harkness and A. J. Forward. In Medicine we claim many who got their preliminary training here: such as Drs. McIntyre, McLean, Howard Elliot, John Gray, Allan McIllmoyll, Robert Collison, William Munro, Andrew Harkness and Anderson. Messrs. H. H. Ross, Moses McPherson, James Carman, J. S. Carstairs and John Graham have been Principals of High Schools.

Mr. Ross, who was one of my first pupils, has been deemed worthy to represent his native county in our Dominion Parliament. Some of my old pupils have devoted themselves to the press, one of whom, Mr. William Williams, is an able newspaper correspondent and writer. I always felt the great responsibility laid upon me to help to train the young minds that in after years were to mould the destiny of others and promote the welfare of our country. I ever tried to have their future in view and treat them as ladies and gentlemen, men and women, who in a few years would, like myself, be battling with the great problems of life. The teacher ought not to think his whole duty performed when he has gone through with the prescribed course of study, but by example and precept strive to build up in the mind and heart of his pupils a noble manhood.

During my time in this school, the old methods of discipline had not yet given place to the better mode of these days. Still, I can say that but very seldom did I use the birch. I found, that when a boy who was inclined to give trouble to his teacher, entered our orderly school and found himself among those who respected themselves and their school, he soon caught the infection of good manners. And I believe the converse to be true, that a well-inclined boy, when thrown among rude and ill-governed fellow students, will soon fall to their level. My discipline, I know, was considered at the time rather severe by some, but in after years these same aggrieved boys expressed their regret for their conduct, and are to-day among my best friends. I believe that the average boy really desires his teacher to be strict in his discipline. If he sees that his teacher is prompted in his teaching and discipline by a strong interest in his pupils, the boy will appreciate the motive and will honor his master. I can remember but two whom I was obliged to report to the Board for expulsion. The world moves, and education and educational equipments have greatly changed since 1860. Then we had fewer subjects to teach; when these were well taught and mastered I am not sure but that the results were just as satisfactory as they are to-day. I am firmly convinced that we have too many subjects now taught in both Public and High Schools. With fewer subjects, the work of both teacher and pupil can be concentrated, and more thorough work secured.

When about half my twenty-six years had elapsed, drawing, music and drill were made optional, and an additional grant was given when they were taken up. Mrs. (Rev.) Blair was engaged to give instruction in object-drawing, and was paid the fees thus obtained. Mr. Forward was employed to visit the school once a week to teach the whole school vocal music; and Mr. T. S. Edwards, without pay, taught military drill.

Physical exercise and calisthenics have been introduced since my time. The law did not demand a reference library or a laboratory. The school raised a nice sum of money by entertainments and spent it on works of reference. The only chemical apparatus we ever had was a set costing about $18.00, procured by myself. During the last ten years of my connection with the school, the Trustees had the power to demand from the Village Council money for putting the school on a good working basis. But for reasons which I shall not here specify, we were compelled to struggle along as best we could with an old, uncomfortable building and no equipment worthy of the name. I trust you will not charge me with selfish egotism in saying that, in spite of all these impediments, the old school continued well attended and stood well in the examinations. At one of the examinations under the new law, twenty wrote for third-class certificates, and twenty passed. We sent at one time four candidates to McGill College for matriculation, and received great praise for their good standing from the Montreal press.

During that quarter of a century we had among the Trustees several men besides the six I mentioned before, who exerted a powerful influence for good in behalf of the school. Dr. Stephenson,

Dr. Steacy (of Mountain), Dr. Williams, Dr. Cowan, Mr. Robert Toye, Solomon Doran, Dr. Colquhoun, and others. They seemed to consider the welfare of the Grammar School equal in importance to their own private business. Often did I go to J. S. Ross, or William Elliot, or Philip Carman with my troubles, and ever received their advice and sympathy.

In the earlier years of my headmastership, the Rev. Mr. McKenzie, a Church of England clergyman, was the sole inspector for the province. He was a man of small size, but of large mind and of a most kindly heart. His death caused a vacancy that was filled by the appointment of two inspectors—Messrs. Marling and Buchan. This was made necessary by the increase in the number of High Schools, and the greater thoroughness of inspection that was now instituted. On the death of Mr. Buchan, Dr. McLellan became one of the inspectors. Mathematics was the favorite subject of the new inspector, and for some years it was the *bête noir* of candidates in what was termed at that time the intermediate examinations. Other subjects were of comparatively small importance. The papers first set were of so difficult and catching a character, that but few succeeded throughout the province. I deem it a most mischievous course to permit any man to impose his own pet subject on the schools, and thus consign English, Classics or Science to an undeserved neglect. After Mr. Marling's death and Dr. McLellan's transference to another position, the present men—Messrs. Hodgson and Seath—became inspectors.

My connection with the High School closed with the year 1885, and I have no reason to blush at the results in the examinations of my last years and of the succeeding July examination. Some may possibly think that I am wanting in good taste to thus refer to my own work. My justification is that erroneous and unfair comparisons have been made during the past ten years. I rejoice that we have now this fine building, a large and well-selected reference library, a first-class science equipment, and four good teachers. Surely we are justified in expecting large results from so great an outlay. I hope that Iroquois will have no reason to regret the great sacrifices that she has made, by which she has somewhat atoned for the neglect of earlier years.

You can readily imagine how the school, its grounds, its familiar old building, which often got the appellation of "The Seminary," the sound of the bell, the rooms and all became dear to me in all those 26 years. On the last day, when I had bidden good-bye to the pupils, I tarried behind to think over the past and say good-bye alone to the mute scenes of past labor. The causes and circumstances of my leaving the school are well known to you all. I refuse to mar the pleasure of this occasion by discussing them ; I have no occasion to blush for my part in the difficulty.

And now in closing these rambling reminiscences, I do so with the hope that the present staff and pupils may be inspired with a greater love for the school that has a half-century of history, and that the heritage entrusted to them may be the more highly appreciated from this day's celebration.

GREETINGS.

BY JAMES A. CARMAN, B.A.

I very gladly avail myself of the opportunity afforded in the invitation given me to send words of greeting to this jubilee meeting to-day. For the expatriated *boys* and *girls* of the old High School, whether our lot is cast beside the Pacific, amid the attractions of the Golden State, whether we climb the rugged steeps and breathe the pure air of the Rockies, whether we wander over the prairie country, wherever we may be, for us there is always a charm in visions of the St. Lawrence Valley. Its verdant fields, its fresh foliage, the clear blue-green waters of the great river, the fleets of vessels, the old fishing and boating grounds, are ever present in our memories. To recall their delightful associations stirs within us the liveliest and pleasantest emotions; and next to the hearth in the home of our childhood, the fireside about which we clustered and frolicked as children, where the father presided with genial dignity and joined in the fun, and where our loving mother smiled upon our sports—that childhood home enshrined in all that is kindliest and tenderest in our memories—next to that home comes the *old school*.

On the *old campus* to-day what yarns are being spun by the *old boys* and the *old girls!* I wish I were with you in your reunion. My own first recollection of the old *Seminary* are not among the least lively of my history. I am reminded of the small school-room on the first floor at the south-west end of the old building. This room was not especially elaboraté or elegant in its appointments and furniture, and was occupied by a score or more of pupils, presided over by Mr. Cowan. Among the classes that must have been his especial annoyance, and that used sometimes to occupy seats on the edge of the platform at his feet, was one of two pupils, a boy and a girl—myself and a little girl, who is now an esteemed Iroquois lady, and who doubtless is present to-day. The work of that little class was reading and spelling, and especially exploring the mysteries of addition, and substraction, and multiplication, and division. Small as I was, I occupied a desk which I called my own, and which I could always find, because it had carved on the top in large, legible characters the name *John.* Just back of me sat Andrew Mills and John Oxnam—names that will be familiar to very many present. And what mischief my amateur cranium could not concoct was supplied from behind. I have never forgotten the valentine I wrote my class-mate, and have often wished I had a copy of it.

And we were pupils of the secondary school of that day! The scope and character of the work in that school may be estimated. Doubtless others of the twenty or twenty-five of Dr. Cowan's charge were soon to matriculate at Victoria or McGill, or at Toronto.

A striking contrast, this school to-day with its modern language specialist, its mathematical expert, its classical devotee, its elaborately equipped science department, and its specially-trained science instructor; its museum, its library, and its well-furnished and commodious school-rooms.

And this school is only one of the many institutions of its class scattered over Ontario. These, in many cases, have been developed from like modest beginnings, and have been evolved under the Ontario school system—an educational system justly the pride of Canadians, since the schools are doubtless at least equal to any on the continent. This excellence has been attained by steady and wise advances, until the pupil of the present enjoys privileges and advantages that would have been marvels and wonders, educationally, in our school days. While all this is true, is there not ground for the suspicion that, to some extent at least, the work of the Ontario schools is *machine work*, and that the product smacks of the *factory?*

It is all very well for the professor of pedagogics, and the psychologist and the psychophysicist to look with supercilious air toward the days of the ferule, of the log school-house and of the grotesque country school teacher. Did not the true-hearted, earnest, ingenious teacher, often amid unfavorable surroundings, succeed in instilling and stirring up an interest that produced fine results in the development and culture of the pupils in his charge?

With all the advantages of modern methods does it seem so certain that educational results are so decidedly in advance? How do the reading habits and tastes of ourselves compare with those of our fathers and grandfathers? Were they not quite as apt to read and appreciate a good book as we? Locally, provincially, nationally are our leading men in public places broader, larger, better educated, in the true sense of the term, than Canadians in similar positions have been for a few generations back?

I simply suggest. I do not depreciate nor undervalue what has been and is being accomplished, but it has seemed to me sometimes that the *forms* and theories, and *ists* and *isms*, and *straight jackets* were in danger of quenching, or at least of hampering and discouraging, true educational enthusiasm.

BY JOHN S. CARSTAIRS, B.A.

Mr. Chairman and Ladies and Gentlemen,—When my old friend and mentor, Adam Harkness, Esq., the Chairman of the Celebration Committee, told me that I should be the first of the speakers to-day, I remarked, "That's quite right, for, you know, there is always some random shooting and skirmishing before the battle begins; skirmishers first and heavy artillery afterwards." "No," he replied, "that isn't it at all; we put you in the front of the battle on the principle of 'Old men for counsel and young men for war.'"

And, Ladies and Gentlemen, whether as a light skirmisher, or as the front man in that honorable vanguard of the *alumni* of Iroquois High School that she has been for fifty years pouring into the lap of Canada, I hope I am fully sensible of the honor that is done me to-day—sensible, not only on my own account, which may seem very natural to you, but also on your account, which may seem somewhat ambiguous to you and egotistic on my part. But we shall speak of that later.

I feel this honor on my account because of all the associations that cluster for me around the very name of Iroquois High School. No matter what I might be able to say concerning that grand old institution, were my capabilities increased tenfold, I should be merely giving back to her in shower what I gathered here in vapor and sunshine. It matters not whether it be the old hospitable stone structure that our forefathers built for us out of their wisdom and self-denial, and consecrated with their unerring foresight, or the magnificent massive building that a later generation has provided; it is to the institution itself—the *alma mater* which has reflected so much credit on our community, which has been such a factor for good throughout the Dominion—that my affection clings. Each building, the old and the new, has its own golden chain of memories, unalloyed by baser metal. The old building again comes up before me with its long rows of windows peeping out from the dense foliage of the maples, denser now by the growth of sixteen years. In its south-west corner, in an upper chamber, I first investigated the mysteries of the hieroglyphic numerals; the same corner saw the agonies of my first efforts in penmanship. Thus, as a student, I was born there. Years passed away, I had seen other schools, and at the age of sixteen I again found myself a pupil within the walls of our old High School.

I often look back at that epoch in my life with thankfulness. Sixteen is the most plastic period of a boy's life. The kindly counsel and ever-ready assistance of Mr. Whitney and his able colleagues, Mr. Alex. McLeod and Mr. J. M. Kinney, stimulated in me a love and thirst for knowledge and exact scholarship that has always been, that always will be, with me. We were a happy family, and the discipline of the school was simply the discipline of the family. To me, even now, with the wider knowledge that comes with a teaching experience extending over fifteen years, our school life of the late 70's seems in many respects an ideal school-life.

Our reading-room, well-stocked with papers, furnished recreation when weather or inclination led us to reject football, cricket, or baseball. Our Literary and Debating Society won fame in the local press as "The Lime-Kiln Club," and once blossomed out into a dramatic concert, that scored a prodigious success in Iroquois and netted sixty dollars for the founding of a High School library. But in Cardinal, alas! Our concert met failure, a rainy night, muddy roads, a breakdown, sore feet from the long walk home and sore hearts from a newspaper controversy that followed. However, we netted fifteen cents for our infant library fund.

If such were our more serious pleasures, we were not without our more frivolous pastimes. Of course, the superfluity of animal spirits would effervesce in tricks. Our northern boundary was not marked by a fence in those days, and we assumed a control over stray cattle for which no by-law granted us authority: horses and cows were started out from the north-west angle of the school with tin-pail attachments that goaded them to a speed at which their owners marvelled. What the owners said is scarcely worth mentioning here. There was an initiation ceremony for every new pupil. It was in the school when I came; it was there when I left. For the first several days of his High School life, the novice was "elevated," as it was technically called, on strong arms and tossed upward as in a blanket, until he touched those old, time-stained cross-beams of the roof; the number of hoists being always tempered to the non-resistance of the victim. Of course, the public generally, and the teachers in particular, were not "cordially invited to be present" at these demonstrations.

But whether we were reading Herodotus or working out *sines* and *cosines*, I feel now that the methods were sane and that the work was that of the true teacher. For many years after, during that period of transition from the microcosm of the school-room to the macrocosm of the world—those salad-days required for the schoolboy to adapt himself to the larger circumstances, of which we teachers fondly hope we are making our schools the miniature image; —during these days of disappointment and sometimes of triumph, my Herodotus, my Mathematics, my Macaulay, " were old friends never seen with new faces, the same in wealth and in poverty, in glory and in obscurity,"—my consolation in adversity, my confidants in prosperity. What school, what teacher can have a higher aim, can accomplish a greater work than to widen the sources of human happiness and implant a love of learning? Education is but "a sounding brass and a tinkling cymbal" if it passes candidates at examinations, yet leaves them without "Onward, onward!" branded deep into their hearts.

Such was the life and spirit of Iroquois High School in 1879 and 1880, in which I participated, first as a pupil, and later as a pupil teacher. The leading boys often talked of the day when we should celebrate the "Golden Wedding" of the school. Fifteen years have scattered them over the whole North American Continent. One is carrying the Gospel, in the intervals of his farm labors, to the settler and savage that nestle at the foot of the Rockies; three are handling the scalpel and dispensing health, one in a large city of the West, the other two in neighboring counties; another trio are lawyers, one in the Western States, a second in the capital of the Dominion, and the third here among you,—the two latter greatly contributing to the success of to-day's meeting—an eighth is laying out new settlements with chain and theodolite in the prairies of the West; and the speaker is the ninth. Those nine boys, now "severed far and wide by mountain, stream, and sea," played and hoped and struggled here in the miniature school world only fifteen years ago. This is but the merest glimpse at the influences that were set in motion by this grand old school during the three years that I was connected with it. Did the Carmans and Coonses build wisely and well?

Ten years passed before I was again connected with my *alma mater*. Changes had taken place: an *alumnus* of the school had been five years her principal; the old school-building had become but a memory; a new building with complete equipment, had superseded the old establishment; a hundred busy pupils filled the new class-rooms. And the same old spirit was hers still. The school had expanded. A native product had succeeded so surpassingly as principal, that perhaps the Board was impelled to offer to me, though only a foster-child of Iroquois, a position on the staff. Those times are recent; no halo of the past has gathered round them; yet I can be pardoned for speaking of them when it is remembered that it is as the representative of the James A. Carman *regime* that I have been invited to this platform to-day. To the three C.'s of that period, Carman, Casselman, and Carstairs, those days are sacred. The staff and school were a unit. Not one misunderstanding, not one harsh word or thought clouds the brightness of those golden associations. We met almost as strangers, we parted life-long friends, that neither time nor distance can sever.

The school was large; our energies were taxed almost to the utmost. In one year one hundred and seventy pupils were enrolled. The junior classes were very large, constituting from one-half to two-thirds of the whole school; the senior classes alone went up for examinations. Thus, examinations were a gauge of merely a part, the smaller part of the actual work done; but, as you will remember, those examination results were always very fair, and often excellent. But in that work for which rubbing against the world is the only examination,—in that culture of the *mens sana et sanum corpus*, the school was in no respect deficient. The discipline was based wholly on the self-respect of the pupil. During the three years I was Classical and English Master of Iroquois High School, but one case of severe discipline arose. I was responsible for it, and I do not regret it. The public spirit of the pupils was so strong and so healthy that I never knew a mark to deface the school premises; every breakage was reported, generally voluntarily, and provided for on individual responsibility. The social life issued in a Boys' and in a Girls' Literary Society, both of a very high character. These two societies often combined under a teacher's supervision, and formed a centre for socials, concerts, conversats, and public debates, which were deserving of the liberal patronage you gave them. Boys and girls alike developed excellent powers as public speakers and organizers.

At the close of 1891, Mr. Casselman and I resigned; Mr. Casselman to accept the position of Drawing Master in the Provincial Normal School at Toronto, and I to complete my University course at the University of Toronto. On graduation I was reappointed to my old position; at the same time a fourth teacher was appointed to the staff in the person of Miss Ida Dillabough, a young lady who is still a member of the staff, and whose industry, faithfulness and ability have added greatly to the reputation and teaching power of the school. The fall of 1892 was notable also for a series of attacks on everything relating to the High School, the Chairman, the Principal, the Classical-master, individual Trustees, the Board as a whole. The very existence of the school seemed menaced. Of these I shall not speak, but this is certain, that if John A. Carman founded the school in 1846, his son, James A. Carman, rendered it the very greatest possible service in 1892.

In July, 1893, Mr. Carman retired, owing chiefly to a severe physical affliction, and I accompanied him. He has left here with us, living in a thousand hearts, a record for manly straightforwardness, sanity of teaching method, thorough honesty of purpose, surpassing prudence and surpassing power of organizing that are not often found combined in one man.

> "His life was gentle; and the elements
> So mixed in him that Nature might stand up,
> And say to all the world, 'This is a man.'"

Every week that I pass here on the old spot of our boyhood, some of our old pupils will call and confide in me how much they owe to having come in contact with the sterling, manly character of James A. Carman. Truly his

> ". . . echoes roll from soul to soul,
> And *grow* forever and forever."

APPENDIX.

I have already said that I feel it an honor to address you to-day, not merely on my own account but also on yours. I have lived much among you, as well as much away from you; I have had frequent opportunities of knowing how great an interest you take in education. My contact with other communities has led to comparisons, and you have never suffered in this respect. You support schools liberally—very liberally; you encourage all educational and educative enterprises with your purse and your presence. Where can you find in all Ontario another municipality of the size of Matilda township, that furnishes so many High School pupils? Though your schools may be burdensome, in no place have I found so many citizens ready and willing to discuss educational matters rationally. This is well, but let me utter a note of warning: "Do not grow self-complacent; do not say we are a nice people; we have the finest educational system in the world; we may sit down and let the system run itself." Constant vigilance is the price of safety in matters educational, as well as in matters military.

But I have tried to find an explanation of this local yet widespread abiding interest in education that is so marked a characteristic of your community; and I have believed that I find it in the very occasion and men we celebrate to-day. For fifty years the conscious and unconscious factors of a well-conducted educational institution have been going out among you; an institution founded on self-denial, maintained through self-sacrifice, and thus enhanced a thousand-fold in your estimation. For fifty years you have had the men themselves that founded and sustained this institution, going in and out among you—no mean educative factor! For fifty years you have had the influences that such men set in motion, accumulating like the avalanche as it sweeps down the mountain-side; yet, unlike the avalanche, an accumulation of benign and blessed elements. Can you question the result?

Fifty years ago, Iroquois was not much. There were three stores, two hotels, the post-office and the steamboat landing. Down near the gravel road was the Laing store, with a little settlement around it; and up the river was Mr. Jacob Brouse's store. Near the steamboat landing was the first stone school-house ever built in the county, which was recently torn down to make way for a meat market. Here fifty pupils used to assemble, one of whom is the speaker of the day, Rev. Dr. Carman, General Superintendent of the Methodist Church. The teacher was Mr. John J. Kerr.

Already in 1843 the Trustees, Mr. Philip Carman, Mr. Geo. Brouse, Mr. Chas. E. Rose, were asking the Government Superintendent of Education, concerning the steps necessary to erect their school into a grammar school. Their efforts in this direction failing, Mr. John A. Carman built a substantial stone edifice at his own expense on land given by Messrs. James and Matthew Coons, and presented it to a Board in trust for posterity.

To appreciate the true significance of this act of Mr. Carman, let us look at the condition of education in Canada in 1846. When the school was opened, Egerton Ryerson, the founder of our common school system was travelling in Europe, and had not yet been commissioned Superintendent of Education two years. When the school was opening in June, 1846,—the first abiding touch of Ryerson's hand, on our common school system, the embodiment of his researches and experiences among the educational systems of Europe— I mean, the Act of 1846—was passing through the Legislature under the management of the Hon. W. Draper. In 1846 Victoria University was ten years old, Queen's five, Toronto three ; and Trinity and Albert were yet unborn. The Iroquois school preceded the first issue of the first educational paper, *The Journal of Education*, and the first County Convention of teachers, by a year. It was in 1846 that Dr. Ryerson issued his first circular to Municipal Councils. Fifty years ago, then, we had not one Public school as we understand the term, we had no educational journals, no teachers' meetings, no Normal schools, and but three infant universities. Less than fifty years ago, we could find an enlightened Chairman of an Education Committee offering such a resolution as this, and the Gore District Council, meeting at Hamilton, adopting it :

"With respect to the necessity of establishing a Normal with elementary
"Model School in this Province, your memorialists are of the opinion that,
"however well-adapted such an institution might be to the wants of the old
"and densely populated countries of Europe, where services in almost every
"vocation will scarcely yield the common necessaries of life, they are, so far
"as the object expected to be gained is concerned, *altogether unsuited to a*
"*country like Upper Canada*. . . . Nor do your memorialists hope to
"provide qualified teachers by any other means in the present circumstances
"of the country than by securing, as heretofore, the service of those *whose*
"*physical disabilities* from age render this mode of obtaining a livelihood the
"only one suited to their *decayed energies*, or by employing such of the *newly*-
"*arrived emigrants* as are qualified for common school teachers, year by year,
"as they come amongst us, and who will adopt this as a means of temporary
"support until their character and ability are known and turned to better
"account for themselves."

Mr. James Little, Chairman of the Gore Educational Committee, certainly deserves fame ! But *de mortuis nihil nisi bonum.*

A little more than fifty years ago there were only twenty-five Grammar Schools in all Upper Canada, educating 958 pupils at an annual cost of $16,320. To-day our two largest Collegiate Institutes have more pupils, while many of our High Schools have a larger expense account. And yet here, in a modest and unassuming settlement in a cedar swamp on the banks of the St. Lawrence, there was a modest and unassuming man (we all remember him) who, of his own free will, without Government assistance, or the hope of Government assistance, impelled merely by that manly and practical philanthropy that marked his life, built the commodious and substantial structure of our boyhood, deeded it to posterity and brought to our doors the blessings of education in a generation that was notably the most ignorant and illiterate, owing to its unfortunate circumstances, that Canada had yet seen.

When the Matilda County Grammar School set sail in June, 1846, it was a wholly private enterprise; there was the possibility but not the promise of Government assistance. The "Seminary," as it was called even in my boyhood, had a piano-room and sleeping apartments upstairs, class-rooms and a residence for the principal downstairs. The school was well equipped, and possessed appliances not often seen, even to-day, in our more modern establishments. A piano was bought by private subscription, and in my school-days I saw the remains of what must have been a very complete tellurian, giving an objective representation of the whole solar system.

I am led to believe that in all Upper Canada there were not six Grammar School buildings that surpassed it in size, appearance and stability; none that surpassed it in accommodation.

Such, then, is the debt that we owe to that generation of Carmans, Coonses, Roses and Brouses, locally. They must impress us all as men living long before their time. Scattered over Canada, over the United States, are thousands, with their children and children's children, whom their wise foresight has blessed. I had thought when I assumed my duties in Stirling that I was a stranger in a strange place; yet here I find two of our old High School pupils preceding me. And yet to the Carmans of that generation Ontario at large owes another and greater educational debt. They must have felt that in Matilda Grammar School they had built wisely and well, for we find both Philip and John A. Carman among the Trustees of the Belleville Seminary, applying for an Act of incorporation as a University.*

In conclusion, how are we fulfilling the educational obligations that such men as these have laid upon us? We support our schools liberally. Does our duty cease there? We attend educational meetings; are these all in all? We certainly cannot lay much claim to the self-sacrificing educational activity that so abundantly characterized the founders of the old "Matilda County Grammar School," as they called it.

It seems to me that our first aim should be to set a high educational standard, and to bend everything to that standard. That standard must reach the wayside cottage, the home of the nation at large. Froude remarks that the United States places as its standard, that every citizen born has a fair and equal start in

---

* Rev. Dr. Carman writes: "The charter was obtained as Belleville Seminary in 1857, and, I presume, was obtained soon as sought. In 1866, it was erected, by enlarged charter, into a University with powers in Arts; and, in 1871, by charter, still further enlarged into a University with full powers in all Arts and Faculties."

life. Everyone knows that he has a chance of becoming President of the Republic. This has made at least a "pushing" race, we must admit. Knox gave Scotland a system of Parochial Schools that sought nothing higher than to teach man's duty to God and man. We know the nation that "the land of brown heath and shaggy wood," as a result, has sent forth to every land. Where are our standards? Do either of these Scottish principles form a portion of our school code?

Not long ago a teacher in a neighboring High School asked his pupils whether they wished an education or a certificate at the coming departmental examinations. All but one answered, "A certificate!" This incident indicates to me a very unhappy tendency to confuse the means and the end; a tendency to forget that there is *an* education and there is *the* education. *An* education may give you certificates, it may give you the insignia of scholarship; *the* education goes deeper: it wakens every faculty, quickens every power, and, in the words of Herbert Spencer, gives "the right ruling of conduct in all directions under all circumstances." *The* education will send forth our boys and girls equipped, not merely with certificates, but with live intelligence and strong characters.

Far be it from me to utter a jeremiad against the educational tendencies of our secondary schools—I am no pessimist—but I do feel that the High Schools are not fulfilling the hopes of their founders. I feel that the masses pay for the High Schools, and that the High Schools are fast becoming mere technical schools for the partial training of teachers and other professional men. I feel that the High School Entrance Examination is a thick-set hedge; the Public School Leaving Examination a "thicker-set" hedge, in which there are no gaps. As a result, a large class of our young men and women, who could profit by the complete appliances of our schools, and the high scholarship of the teachers, who, moreover, are paying a large proportion of the cost of these institutions—are yearly shut out from these advantages. They may not wish to qualify for a profession, but they might, and could, qualify better for life. If the education we are dispensing is a good for the professional class, surely a portion of it at least should be a good for the sons and daughters of our farmers and mechanics who have no professional ambitions. We have no more right to close our High Schools against the mendicant in Arithmetic or the unfortunate in Spelling, if otherwise qualified in maturity and intelligence, than to close our churches against the mendicant in pocket. And herein we have one of our most terrible wastes of educational force and power. Instead of being close corporations, our High Schools should be as they were, I believe, twenty years ago, centres of educational light, sending forth their beams on all that have outgrown in knowledge and intelligence the average pupil of the district school; centres, from which shall pour forth a constant stream of influences that shall raise the general level of intelligence. And we need not fear to reach the high-water mark too soon.

If we are thus falling in our educational ideals from those of our fathers in our duty to man, where do we stand in teaching our duty to the Great Architect of the Universe? Our Bibles are good one day in the week, how about the other six days? Our Roman Catholic fellow-citizens are at least consistent as a Christian people and an historic Christian Church, when they insist on religious instruction in their schools. Are we consistent, boasting our Protestantism, boasting an open Bible, and pluming ourselves on a more enlightened faith; yet, trusting to chance to instruct our children in Biblical facts—facts, remember, not doctrines? Aside from its paramount claim as a revelation from God to man, aside from its claim as one of our masterpieces of English, the Bible is the earliest history, the earliest biography, the earliest poetry, and the earliest code of ethics of the race. Should not the least of these be a sufficient claim to raise it to the rank of a mere text-book in our schools? A text-book of facts and literature, not necessarily of doctrines, on which to base theological squabbles. No, our Roman Catholic fellow-citizens are right; we are wrong. Let us say so. Let them have religious schools; let us have a school with a Bible. A Christian race without a Bible is an anomaly—an impossibility. For

> "It's the little rift within the lute
> That by-and-by will make the music mute,
>   And, ever-widening, slowly silence all,—
> The little rift within the lover's lute,
> Or little pitted speck in garnered fruit,
>   That, rotting inwards, slowly moulders all."

The first fifty years in the history of this institution have passed away. The men who founded it, the old building, have alike vanished; they made life a less serious problem for us, they made such changes in our environment that a broader intelligence and wider opportunities have beamed upon us. Our duties are plain: to do for posterity at least as much as those grand old men did for us. Let us free our High Schools from the narrow professionalism, with which I fear, only too justly, they may be charged; let us be consistent in our claim of an open Bible, and we shall rear on these shores a nation equal to the Scottish under Knox's system of Parochial Schools; and when the hands of old Time's clock point to 1946, as a second "Golden Wedding" for the old Matilda County Grammar School, perhaps some other gathering of old boys and old girls of the School, who are now unborn, shall give us that least and greatest word of praise possible, "They have done their duty."

SCIENCE IN SCHOOLS.

By John Harkness, M.D.

Forty-one years ago now, I, a boy of thirteen, entered the Iroquois Grammar School, which had just been placed under the charge of Mr. Albert Carman, a young man fresh from college, who, I understood, undertook to run it for the Government grant and what he could make out of fees. The fees were $3.00 per term (four terms in the year) for the English branches, and $4.00 when the classics were included. I had received my preliminary training in a little square log-house, with a window in each side, made long horizontally; one half of which was movable, and around the frames of which and of the door there were generally more or less openings through which daylight could be seen—especially around the door. The inside furnishings consisted of a box stove in the middle of the floor, with a pipe running up straight through the roof, two forms or benches, which could be moved near to or away from the stove, as occasion would require, and around three sides of the house against the wall a desk, with the seat (a continuous board) on the inside, so that we had to step over the seat and sit with our faces to the wall.

In the Grammar School we were taught reading, writing, grammar and geography, with mathematics and classics. During the three years in which Mr. Carman taught and I attended, we had small classes of four or five in astronomy, geology and physiology. This was altogether voluntary on the part of the students and teacher; no provision, so far as I am aware, being made in the curriculum for teaching science. But of late years science, as popularly understood, has a recognized place in our High School course, and I am pleased to say that we have very good facilities for teaching it. I have every expectation that it will have a still more important place in the near future.

The great and most important object of education in our schools is not so much the acquisition of knowledge as the training of the mind to enable it in after life to acquire that knowledge for itself. The transcendent importance of a scientific education for the highest development of life cannot be too strongly insisted upon. Science is organized knowledge. From the moment we open our eyes and wail forth our first cry in this life, we begin the acquisition of knowledge. Every phenomenon of which we take cognizance is a scientific fact, the act of taking cognizance no less than any other. Science arranges all this knowledge in an orderly whole; the orderly arrangement of phenomena most nearly related being a particular science. Each of the sciences has a development of its own, but they all follow a certain course. Somebody groups a number of observations, and perhaps draws an inference or states a hypothesis; somebody else groups another number of facts, and draws a different inference. The antagonism stimulates observation, and after a time, when the progress of knowledge has made the time ripe, a master mind appears, groups all the phenomena, sees their relations, and places them in orderly sequence, and we have a harmonious whole governed by a *law*.

Allow me to illustrate shortly by that most nearly perfect of all the sciences, Astronomy—most nearly perfect, because in it we are able to previse phenomena much more than in any other. And in no other have we a more striking illustration of the value of a *hypothesis* as a working basis. Copernicus propounded the theory of modern astronomy, but it was nothing more with him than a hypothesis without proof. After him, and working on his hypothesis, the accurate and very numerous observations of Tycho Brahe, made for many years, enabled his great pupil, Kepler, after years of profound thought, to establish his three great laws under which the planets move, and to recognize the force of gravitation. The time was now ripe for the completion of the astronomical theorem, and the man appeared in Isaac Newton, who, in his epoch-making work, "Principia," irrefragably established the law that "gravity varies inversely as the square of the distance." This seems to have made astronomical *theory* complete, and all the discoveries and observations made since have been found to conform to these laws.

In the same way Geology was placed on a stable basis about the time of the establishment of this school, by the publication of the successive editions of that wonderful work, Lyell's "Principles of Geology," although the geological text-book which I used forty years ago here still taught cataclysms, with sudden extinction of old species, and sudden creation of new. Thirty-six years ago Botany and Zoology had the same thing done for them by Darwin's "Origin of Species."

Still more recently two other cognate sciences have assumed or are assuming definite shape, "Sociology," or the Science of Society; and "Ethics," or the Science of Conduct. Until of late years it was not thought that these things were subject to scientific treatment, and even now I may be considered heterodox for claiming that morals has any other "reason for existence," than the commands of a superhuman power. The questions are difficult ones to treat scientifically on account of the extreme complexity of the phenomena involved; but an immense number of data have been collected by a great number of observers, and have been more or less methodically arranged; and there is no doubt that the time has arrived for placing both sciences on a broad, firm foundation.

They, above all others, deserve to be taught in our schools, especially Ethics, as it so intimately concerns our daily and hourly life; and I think that a recognition of the distinctive difference between

www.ingramcontent.com/pod-product-compliance
Lightning Source LLC
Chambersburg PA
CBHW030433190426
43202CB00036B/128